I
HELLO AMERICA

"Like Caesar, who said about Gaul… 'Veni, vidi, vici' – so Mary Matuja 'Came, saw, and conquered' America, and all of our hearts in the process."
—Nancy McDonnell, author

"I have always admired and respected Mary Matuja, but those feelings have doubled after reading her wonderful book *Hello America*. The vivid descriptions of her life as a child in war-torn Czechoslovakia are absolutely spellbinding. Mary Matuja is a thoughtful, honest, and diligent public official, and a great American. She is an inspiration to all of us."
—Judge Mark Switalski, Macomb County Circuit Court

"Mary's story is a shining example of hope, hard work, miracles and the American Dream. It is proof that with God, anything is possible."
—Jack Krasula, President of Trustinus, LLC and radio host of *Anything is Possible*

HELLO
AMERICA

A MEMOIR

To Mary + Norm,
My wonderful friends, you
make the world a better place!
just because you're in it!
Love,
Mary

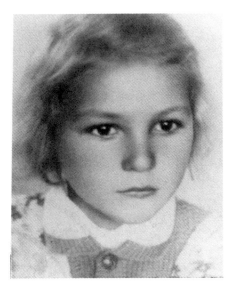

Young Marya

HELLO
AMERICA

A MEMOIR

MARY MATUJA

TWOHARBORS
WWW.TWOHARBORSPRESS.COM

Two Harbors Press
322 First Avenue N, 5th floor
Minneapolis, MN 55401
612.455.2293
www.TwoHarborsPress.com

ISBN-13: 978-1-63413-584-9
LCCN: 2015909187

Distributed by Itasca Books

Edited by Candace Zann

Printed in the United States of America

This book is dedicated to
Grandmother, who gave me discipline
and
Grandfather, who gave me hope.

Acknowledgments

I am grateful to all whose lives have touched and intersected with mine on both continents.

I send my love and gratitude to my daughters, Leslie Wizner, Jennifer Rosa, and Nicole Boutrous, for your encouragement and belief in my ability to finish this story. Without your help of organizing, researching, and cheering me on, I would still be agonizing over the manuscript and ready to give up.

To my grandson, Adam, I send a special thank-you for transcribing the text, written in longhand and sometimes illegible.

To my granddaughter, Taylor, thank you for your special talent in journalism and your keen eye for prose, which inspired me.

Special thanks to my longtime friend Marilyn Moore, who planted the seed to write this memoir many years ago, when our children were attending school in Roseville, Michigan.

Thank you to Aunt Justina Tahla (the cowgirl) and the late Aunt Jevka, for providing valuable information for the book. I am so grateful to both of you. And a big thanks to cousin Gabriel Tahla for corresponding and providing me with photos and documentation. Your updates about our relatives, cousin Haňňa Gal, cousin Mishko, Ĺuba and Marya, who passed away four years ago, will always be remembered. Thank you also to cousin Anne Kuzdac-Wilson for your support.

To my aunts, thank you for your love and kindness throughout my childhood and beyond.

I send my love and gratitude to my editor, Candace Zann. I planted a small, lowly acorn, and you grew a beautiful oak tree. I am thankful for your expertise, wordsmith!

I send my love and a very special thank-you to my husband, Bob, for his unwavering support in enduring my frustrations while I struggled profoundly in the writing of this memoir. Thank you for hanging in there with me.

I want to say thank you to the Utica High School Class of '57 for the continuing journey of your friendship. You have contributed golden threads to the tapestry of my life. With special thanks for your help and encouragement: Earl Schroeder, dubbed our class historian; Carol Parrott Duvall; Shirley Declereq Frederick; Lois Breederland Skibins; Wayne Stewart, our legal eagle; Bob Kreger; Beverly Tipler Ruble; Joyce Faith Kilpatrick; Rita Media Dotter; Walter and Delores (Malburg) Pheil; Bill Webb, my dance partner; Neal Ogden; Denise Kerner Pitzen; Gordon Stough; Ray Van De Weghe; Vince Angel; the late Tom Jankowski; our educators still teaching and praising; Mr. Louis Boggs and wife, Mary; and Mrs. Harriet Robertson (a descendant of President Abraham Lincoln).

Special thanks to: my longtime friend Dorothy Kakarian Busch and her special son, Patrick; Mary Jane Chiodo, who recites the story of my life verbatim—thank you for listening; Geraldine Paddock— fate brought us together; Jan Haggerty, Roseville councilwoman; the late Macomb County commissioner Leonard Haggerty, who taught me how to campaign; Yvonne Smith and the late Marge Morgan, longtime friends and supporters; Mary and Harold Norman; the Martin family and the Holman family; the Angelleli family, the Dr. Jack Kare family, and the Merrelli family, also longtime friends and supporters.

Thank you to Mike Kenyon, former Grosse Pointe Shores City manager, and to Angela Kenyon, for your help during my tenure as supervisor of Grosse Pointe Township and as chairwoman of the Grosse Pointe Shores Planning Commission.

To Mayor Ted J. Kedzierski, Mayor Pro Tem Bruce Bisballe, council members Alexander Ajlouni, Kay Felt, Robert Barrette Jr.,

Robert Gesell, and Daniel Schulte—I say thank you for your vote of confidence in permitting me to serve the village of Grosse Pointe Shores, a Michigan City.

I have had the honor of working with many interesting and talented people. Special thanks to Helen Bai, chairman of the Grosse Pointe Shores Beautification Committee; former mayor, the late Edmund M. Brady Jr.; former mayor John Huetteman III; and former mayor James M. Cooper.

To the employees of Grosse Pointe Shores, I salute your invaluable dedication to the community you serve. Thank you.

I thank John H. Bierbusse, executive director of Macomb/ St. Clair County Michigan Works; and Laura Carne, whose expertise in taking the minutes of the meetings and remembering all of the names is greatly admired.

To the entire Michigan Works Commission and staff, it has been a wonderful journey working with you. Thank you all.

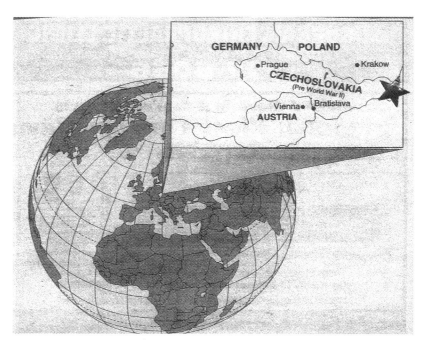

Ćertizne, Czechoslovakia, 1939

Chapter One
The Beginning

Ćertizne, Czechoslovakia—1944

Skipping across the front room toward the kitchen, I stopped by the window. Something drew my attention. Was it a flash of light, a movement? I pushed the white lace curtains aside.

"Baba, Baba! Hurry! Come and see!"

My window perch looked down the hill over the dusty road that was the entrance to our village. There in the distance, my eyes caught a glimpse of sparkles. The sun was shining, and the pretty line of glitter was moving closer.

Again I called to Grandma, "Come and see! Hurry, Baba, hurry!"

Grandma was busily preparing piroshkies in the kitchen. Working quickly, she was boiling the small dough patties stuffed with cheese, potatoes, and sauerkraut. Grandma was making so many delicious dumplings and wrapping them in squares of old cloth. I wondered what holiday celebration was coming up that needed so much food. Annoyed at my continual interruptions, she grudgingly wiped her flour-stained hands on her apron and joined me at the window.

"Look, Baba, look!"

Grandma looked over my head through the clean windowpanes. The expression on her face told me that something was terribly wrong. The sparkles transformed into people walking up the winding dirt road, snaking their way up to the village. The flashes of light that had initially caught my attention had now revealed themselves as reflections off the helmets of the approaching German army.

Without saying a word, Grandma grabbed my arm and hustled me across the room toward the open window. On the other side of the window was our cement porch and below it, our cellar. The porch and cellar beneath were a matter of pride to our family. The cellar was the only one in our tiny village of Ćertizne, and it was hand built by Grandfather. That was to be our destination.

Just as Grandma pulled me through the window, out of the sky came a frightful roar. I looked up to see something bigger than a bird falling from the sky toward our little porch. As it came closer, it brought the sound of rapid gunfire, and bullets pierced the air all around us.

Plunging back into the house through the same open window, Grandma frantically threw me to the floor. She reached over to the bed where Aunt Jevka slept. Then Grandma threw Aunt Jevka's neatly made straw mattress right on top of me. What in the world was Grandma thinking? If that wasn't enough, Grandma threw herself on top of the mattress. Crushed by the mattress and my sturdy Grandma, I was frantic with fear and desperately gasping for air. In my hysterical panic, I started pushing, pulling, and kicking, all at the same time. With all the commotion above us, I was sure Grandma could not hear my garbled sounds of desperation.

In an instant, Grandma jumped up and tossed off the mattress, grabbing and clutching me to her bosom.

"Marya, Marya, breathe, breathe. Inhale, exhale."

Like a sergeant, she ordered me to breathe over and over until my ragged breathing returned to normal. As I calmed down, I sputtered to myself, "If the bullets don't kill me, Grandma and the mattress surely will."

As the gunfire moved away, we started toward the window again. This time we got through the window, slid onto the porch, and jumped off the porch to the ground below. Once on the bare ground, we crawled on our stomachs through twenty feet of dirt to the cellar door.

Just as we reached the locked door, the plane returned, circled, and dove toward us again. Grandma's determined demeanor had now become hysterical as the noise of the plane grew louder. My little fists were pounding the door far below the strong blows of Grandma. Screaming, we begged, "Let us in! Let us in! Let us in!"

Between the hysteria on the inside and the chaos on the outside, the villagers who had already assembled in our cellar below could not tell who was trying to knock the cellar door down. It seemed as though an eternity had passed before the door finally flew open.

Two-year-old Marya with
Grandmother and Aunt Justina

Chapter Two
The Cellar

The open door revealed the wide-eyed inhabitants of our village crammed into the cellar. They looked at us as though they had seen a ghost. They couldn't believe that anyone could have survived the onslaught of the machine guns and bombs they'd heard above.

Grandma pushed our way in. As my eyes adjusted to the dark, I could make out that everyone was here: Grandfather, Great-Grandmother and Great-Grandfather Śafran, Aunt Jevka, Aunt Justina and baby Andreĵ, Uncle Stefan, Aunt Haňňa, Nicolaĵ and Maria, Aunt Kristina with her husband (whom we called "the crane" because of his long neck and gangly legs) and their three children, the Skala family, and other neighbors. All were crammed into our small cellar.

If we organized ourselves just right, there was room for all twenty-five of us to sit down, but room for little else. The children lined up against the four walls. The adults were in the center of the room on their knees, crying and praying for God to save us. I was used to the loud sobs and cries of our family's exaggerated drama, but I could tell right away that this was something different.

Still shaking from the mattress episode and the loud gunfire from the roaring planes, I took my place by the wall with the other children. As I studied the cellar inhabitants, it didn't take long for me to start questioning the arrangement of the room.

"Why do the children have to sit against the wall?" I inquired.

Great-Grandpa Šafran explained, "Dear child, we have lived our lives; it doesn't matter what happens to us. The children will have a better chance of survival if they are along the walls. If the building is bombed, it would probably cave in toward its center."

For one of the first times in my five short years of life, I actually listened to my elders and sat as close as I could against the wall.

The cellar was not only stuffed with people, it was also stuffed with food. In addition to the garden vegetables that we usually stored there, I saw loaves of bread, piroshkies, and containers of polivka (soup). It was early fall, so I expected to see baskets of vegetables in the cellar, but we had never kept Grandma's special cooked meals there. All of the baking and chopping and cooking she had been doing all week were with us down in the cellar. Grandma's hard work was meant to feed this cellar group. In fact, she was retrieving the last batch of piroshkies from the stove when I made my discovery at the window. Grandma had been preparing because she knew the war was imminent.

When Grandma made piroshkies, she attacked the dough with all her might. In her strong hands, the rolling pin was a weapon. She had pitch-black hair worn in a tight bun at the back of her neck. Her head was covered with a black babushka tied under her chin. Her fiery dark eyes peered out and always looked serious. Grandma put the fear of God in me, especially when I did something I shouldn't have, and that was much too often. When it came to discipline, she ruled with an iron hand. No one dared tangle with her.

Grandma, motivated by her perception of duty, always dressed me in her finest creations. She used curtains, old bedspreads, any cloth she could get her hands on. When there was no suitable cloth, our family would make our own cloth.

Aunt Jevka and Aunt Justina would pick the long hemp plants from the fields and carry them to the river in bundles, with babushkas tied around their faces. The long stiff sticks with the five-point leaves swaying on the stalks looked like tiny palm trees. They lugged the bundles down to the river, dunking them in the shallow riverbank and loading rocks on top so they wouldn't float away. The stalks had to be broken down, so it was a constant soaking and beating, soaking and beating. Every time they worked on the hemp, their babushkas were tied tightly around their mouths and faces. They soaked the stalks and then beat the stiffness out of them. Finally, when the stalks became straw-like, they would be dried in the sun.

We would always know when Aunt Jevka and Aunt Justina were hemp picking because they came back home giggling and tipsy. We had no idea that hemp was really a form of marijuana. All we knew was that the aunts never complained when it was time for this chore.

Grandma would then take the soaked and beaten hemp, twist it, and work it into thread. The big loom was set up in the corner of the kitchen for the winter months. When the snows came and the crops were in, Grandma would spend her time making the hemp thread into good, sturdy cloth for her sewing creations. Grandma didn't stop with making my clothing. She knitted, crocheted, and did beautiful petit point as well. But everyone knew the sewing and needlework was always done after the cleaning.

Grandma kept a sparkling house. Floors were swept and scrubbed. Beds were kept neat, and the windows glistened. Grandma's philosophy was, "Cleanliness is next to Godliness." I could never figure this out, especially since Grandma was not too fond of religion or the church.

Down in the cellar with my family and neighbors, I was wearing a pretty, pleated, rusty-brown skirt with a white-ruffled blouse and flesh-tone cotton stockings. Grandma had hand-stitched every tiny pleat in my skirt. She did this even though we had purchased a fancy sewing machine just the year before. On my feet I wore hand-me-down sturdy brown shoes. They were about two sizes too large and stuffed with some rags for a better fit. My outfit was topped off with a ribbon holding a few fine blonde ringlets, tied into a bow on top of my head.

My bow and my bobbed hair were the subject of my frequent fights with Anna Ilkova, a freckle-faced neighbor girl with long red braids. In the darkness of the cellar, I could see her against the opposite wall. Why does she have to be here? I thought to myself. This is our cellar.

Only a few days before, she had been poking fun at my dainty blue bow and bobbed hair.

"You're a snob," she hissed, "like the rich people from Medzilaborce and Bratislava. With your fancy short hair, you think you are too good for us here in Ćertizne."

What she didn't know was that I was jealous of her long thick braids. My hair was not bobbed because I was a snob; it just wouldn't grow. But I couldn't tell her that. So instead, we squabbled. I would pull her braids. She would scratch my face. Occasionally, a thrown stone was involved. But here, stuck against the wall in the cellar with the world exploding above us, our pettiness over our hair would have to wait.

I was glad Grandfather was the leader in the cellar. He was the opposite in temperament and appearance from Grandma. Where Grandma was dark, Grandfather was fair-skinned. He had light brown hair and blue eyes. He was taller than most in our village, standing almost six feet, dwarfing Grandma's short, sturdy frame. While Grandma was hot-tempered and explosive, Grandfather was a mild-mannered gentleman. People admired and respected him. He was kind and caring, always ready to help. I adored him. He was my protector, my hero. Besides that, I could manipulate him much more easily than my suspicious grandma.

As we settled into our new cellar home, it didn't take long before the elders, including Grandfather and Grandma, got together and decided on the many cellar rules. Even though it had been quiet outside for many hours, we were not allowed to venture out until we all clearly understood these rules.

"Under no circumstances are you to leave the property," a stern voice in the corner demanded. We were puzzled. How would we go to the bathroom, since our family outhouse was far from our cellar entrance?

"To relieve yourself, you are to use the bushes and trees near the house," the voice continued. This was not going to be fun at all.

"Never wander beyond this yard into the village." This was repeated several times. I knew it must be an important rule. "And never, ever go out alone," he said. "Better not go out in a group either, because that might draw attention. You may only go out in pairs." That was the final rule. When questioned if we understood, we nodded our heads in unison. All the while, we were trying to remember which rules to follow and agreeing to the terms of our confinement.

Nature eventually called, and I had to go to the bathroom. Grandfather was the other half of my pair and as always, my protector. We were a good team. As we ventured out of the cellar, he let me find my own spot among the bushes to do my business.

Not far off, he called out to me in a soft voice. "Marya, when you are done, go back to the cellar directly," he ordered. "I have to check on something and will be right behind you."

I thought that maybe Grandpa wanted to smoke his pipe because he couldn't smoke it down in the cellar. I answered back, "I will, Grandfather."

But in a flash, my promise to Grandfather was soon forgotten.

Chapter Three

BOOTS

Outside of the crowded, dark cellar, the lavender hills drew me away from Grandfather and his warnings. The tall grasses and wildflowers grew in abundance throughout the meadow and provided a wonderful camouflage as I inched my way up to the top of the hill. Inside the grasses, I could not see ahead, and I could not see behind. It seemed logical to me that if I crawled on all fours, I would be hidden from view. Blindly, I shuffled forward, quickly flattening the ground cover as I passed over it. No one could know that I was on a quest—a quest to discover what lurked in the hills.

Pressing forward, I bumped into something. At first, I thought it might have been a tree trunk, but no, this obstacle was black and shiny. Touching the smooth surface, I realized that I had crawled upon a pair of polished black boots! Gradually, my eyes followed the boots upward, and then my neck craned back. To my amazement, I found myself staring into the cold, steely blue eyes of a stranger. He wore a beautiful uniform, complete with shiny brass buttons and embroidered ribbons on the sleeves. As my eyes continued upward, there, on top of his head was a gleaming metal helmet that sparkled in the sunlight.

My breathing seemed to stop as I was gripped by fear and uncertainty. How was I to get out of this predicament? Grandfather's warnings came flooding back to me, and I suddenly found myself wishing I had heeded them. With determination, I put my head down and as quickly as I had shuffled forward just minutes before, I began withdrawing backward. Maybe I could slip away unnoticed the same way I had come.

However, as I retreated, I collided again—first to the left, then to the right—into other pairs of shiny black boots that blocked my escape. Finally realizing I had been surrounded, I looked up at the crowd that gathered around me. All the men wore the same basic uniforms. Some had colored ribbons and pretty pins above the pockets. Others were stark in their appearance. Then I saw the guns. Large steely weapons of war hung from their shoulders as the soldiers bent down to get a better look at the creature crawling through the grass.

One of the soldiers waved his index finger, motioning for me to get up. I was shaking with fear. I slowly stood up, all the while never taking my eyes off of him. His hand reached for something in his pocket. Thoughts of my demise ran through my mind. My heart stopped. I held my breath. As his hand slipped out, the shine of a bright wrapper surprised me. He carefully removed a chocolata bar! He offered the tantalizing confection to me and I eagerly accepted. And thus began a bittersweet friendship with the enemy.

Wow! What good fortune I had stumbled upon. I tore open the smooth, shiny paper and shoved the sweet confection into my mouth. Within seconds, I had devoured it, leaving only a telltale ring around my mouth. That was delicious, I thought as I licked my lips. I couldn't remember the last time I'd had a treat like that. The men smiled and laughed a bit, uttering a few strange words among themselves. They continued to watch me closely. I, too, kept my eyes on them, wondering when the next chocolata bar would materialize. It seemed an eternity passed as I patiently waited for the soldier's next tasty offering. Sadly, no more chocolate was forthcoming.

By this time, I had remembered the crowd in our cellar. Realizing I could be missed, I turned on my heels and took off like a runaway train down the hill. Running through the knee-high grasses, I crossed to the low ground cover of Uncle Stefan's yard and headed straight for our underground cellar. Unbeknownst to me, my chocolate benefactors were watching me, eagerly waiting for me to reveal our hideout.

When the door opened at my pounding, I faced a group of stern and angry faces. Spotting the chocolate mess on my face, the interrogation began. Never did they guess where I got the chocolate, and I certainly didn't volunteer the story. Once again, I was admonished and forbidden to venture into the hills. However, this time the words came with a much stronger warning.

Nevertheless, almost as soon as I had taken my seat against the wall, I began plotting my next escape. The dampness in the cellar couldn't compare to the joys found in the countryside. It took patience and time, but two days later, opportunity knocked again.

As some of the children left the compound to use the bathroom, I acted fast. Tucked safely behind Haňňa with the beautiful braids, I snuck out, undetected by my grandparents. It is amazing the bravery (or perhaps stupidity) that chocolate will conjure up in a child. This time, instead of crawling on all fours, I simply ran up the hill in plain view. Boldly, I stood at the edge of the hill and waved to my new acquaintances. They waved back, motioning for me to come down to where they were standing. That was all the encouragement I needed. I didn't bother to walk or run; that seemed too inefficient a mode of transportation. Instead, I sat on my bottom and slid down the hill at a furious pace. The lure of chocolata was too great to resist.

As I came to a screeching halt in front of my newfound soldier friends, they proceeded to give me a standing ovation (which, of course, I mistook as a cue to perform). As they clapped, I began to dance, making little circles and twirling around and around as fast as my skinny little legs would carry me. My singing of a favorite made-up tune immediately caught on. It wasn't long before everyone joined in, clapping, singing, and laughing. A good time was had by all, and I was the entertainment. At last, the moment I had been patiently waiting for finally arrived: a chocolata bar appeared.

I smiled and licked my lips in anticipation. I tried in vain to thank them for the chocolate. Once again, I devoured the confection and immediately wiped my face clean with my sleeve. This time, I assured myself, I would not be caught with a tattletale mouth.

Now that my sweet tooth had been satisfied, I paused for a moment to take a look around. My eyes widened as I gazed at a battery of weapons. Even though I had no idea what the strange machines were, they were frightening to me. They looked like giant iron monsters sitting in our fields. I suddenly realized that my new friends, who had generously sweetened my visit with chocolate, also brought real danger.

In that very moment, out of the corner of my eye, I saw my grandfather cresting the hill. My party with the soldiers was abruptly interrupted by Grandfather's unmistakable look of anger. This was a side of him I did not often see, and I knew it meant big trouble. It was too late to run and hide, so I waited, frozen to the spot, as Grandfather approached.

To my astonishment, Grandfather spoke directly to the soldiers in a strange tongue that I had never heard before. When did he learn to speak like that? Although I hadn't the slightest idea what they were saying, the tone in which they spoke was not one of anger. Sensing the situation was not as perilous as I originally had thought, I started planning my escape. Perhaps if I stayed quiet, they would forget about me, and I could slither away undetected. I stood by, sheepishly fidgeting with my skirt and twisting back and forth, figuring out how to make my retreat.

Then, pausing in his conversation, Grandfather turned to me. "Dear child, why do you make such a nuisance of yourself and bother these nice people?" he scolded. This was hardly the rage I was expecting from him.

Nonetheless, sensing I was still in trouble, I immediately tried to soften Grandfather's reproach and kept repeating, "I'm sorry, Grandfather. I'm sorry. I won't do it again."

It all seemed very confusing to me. I didn't think I had been bothering these nice men. They welcomed me each time I paid them a visit. After all, hadn't they rewarded me with chocolata?

It was miraculous that Grandfather knew how to speak the German language and that he had something to talk with the soldiers about – me. The officer with the chocolata who had taken a liking to me told my grandfather that I reminded him of his own daughter. From the same pocket that had held the chocolata he now slipped out a tattered photograph to show my grandfather. There were two smiling girls with blonde hair in the photo, and I wanted to see it. As I was straining my neck to see, the officer brought it down to my level.

Grandfather wisely took this opportunity not only to remark at how much we looked alike but he also told the soldiers my story. My mother was in America, you see, waiting for my arrival, when war broke out. Now he and his wife were left with the responsibility of caring for and protecting this precocious granddaughter. That was the moment that saved our lives. These two men of different backgrounds and generations had something in common. The German soldier and my grandfather shared their worries for children—children far away from their parents.

The officer spoke in a hushed voice. He told Grandfather of the imminent danger to come as the rest of the occupying forces arrived. He could warn us, but only once. Both were whispering now, and Grandfather and the officer hatched a plan. Before I knew it, Grandfather was tugging my arm and dragging me over the crest and down the hill. Stumbling to keep up, I was shocked at Grandfather's ferocity. Once again, my breath was taken away.

This is the area where I encountered the shiny black boots

Chapter Four
THE KNOCK

When we returned to the cellar, life was as we had left it. The villagers were still huddled together in the dark, discussing possibilities and munching on cold potatoes. No one had even missed us. Grandfather interrupted the chatter, hushed the group, and anxiously began to tell of my adventure and to outline the plan.

"We are fortunate that Marya makes friends easily," Grandfather started. "One of her admirers has offered to help us. The German army will soon join the small group of scouts who are occupying the nearby fields, and then this cellar and the village will no longer be safe."

He told everyone about the big machines and the coming soldiers and my dancing for the officer with the two daughters. Everyone was silent. It was their turn to have their breath taken away. Grandfather continued to explain the plan that he and my soldier friend had created. We were to expect a knock on the door, and the messenger would briefly point in the direction for us to travel. That knock would mean we must leave and travel in the direction of the pointed finger. That was it—a mere knock and a gesture. It didn't seem like much, hardly enough to plan our large group's escape, but enough it would have to be.

Grandfather continued, "We must be ready—ready to leave immediately without hesitation and with silence. We must sleep fully dressed, with even our shoes and coats on."

That night, the gathering began. We could take with us only what we could carry and still move quickly. Some of the villagers returned to their homes to collect those items they needed and could carry. What to take? Food was first—potatoes, bread, and fruit off the trees. Then we gathered pots and pans, shovels, rope, and a few other tools. Along with all of these necessities, I saw Aunt Justina huddled in the cellar, clutching her sewing machine.

Within a few anxious days, the dreaded knock came. It was the middle of the night. The bang broke the silence, and the adults jerked up in panic. Baba shook me and told me to quickly follow Aunt Justina. Aunt Jevka carried baby Andrej, a mere sixteen months old. These were the women in charge of keeping track of me. There was confusion and fear in the cellar, as most of the adults ran around trying to grab food, clothing, and anything they could carry.

Grandfather was at the door with the chocolata officer. The officer spoke two words in German and pointed his finger in the direction that we were to travel. Grandfather thanked this soldier who had risked his own life by warning us. He clearly would have been shot had it been discovered that he showed us our escape. We would always remember his kindness, especially whenever we shared chocolata.

And then, we ran into the darkness.

The sewing machine Aunt Justina simply couldn't leave behind

Chapter Five
THE ESCAPE

In the darkness of night, trying to stay together yet running as fast as we could, our group silently pushed into the forest. When I saw a glimpse of the officer at the door to our cellar, I was actually hoping for one more chocolata! I held back and wondered if I would be able to see him. But Aunt Justina yanked my arm and dragged me, and I stumbled behind her. We ran for miles in complete darkness. Since I was one of the youngest members of the group, I was always tripping and falling and wishing I could just lie down and go to sleep. All the while, my aunts were prodding me to move faster.

Trying to keep up with my grandparents and aunts was no easy task. I walked as fast as my little feet would carry me. It must have been the rainy season, because the ground was extremely wet, and at one point in our journey, I happened to step into a deep, muddy sinkhole. It felt like quicksand, sucking me down until I was almost knee-deep. I struggled to get out and when I could no longer move, I cried out for help. Grandma came to my rescue. She pulled and tugged and twisted me from side to side, trying to free me from the pull of the mud. She gave me one last yank and—whoosh—my feet were uncorked from my shoes! As far as I know, my shoes are still buried in that dark and sticky mud hole.

Now what was to be done with this shoeless, whimpering five-year-old kid full of mud? Never fear; Grandma's here! With the authority of a drill sergeant and the precision of an acrobat, she snatched the babushka off Aunt Justina's head and wrapped and tied it around my foot and calf.

Then she proceeded to take off her own babushka to do the same with my other foot. And because they were trying to keep my makeshift boots dry, every member of our family had to take a turn carrying me. First Grandma carried me, and then Grandfather took his turn as well. The young Aunt Justina missed her turn because she was still dragging the sewing machine behind her, cradled in a tarp. Bent over and struggling the whole way, she would not part with that machine. When Aunt Sophie had her turn carrying me, she made it a point to discover drier land. Once there, she plopped me down on the ground to walk, babushka boots and all. No more free rides for me.

The sounds in the forest were scary, especially at night. I could hear owls hooting and the horrible howling sounds of the wolves. Adding in the wind rustling through the trees, it felt like someone was chasing us. I hung onto Aunt Sophie's hand, fearing the wolf would snatch me away and eat me.

Our silent passage in the forest was a time of fearfulness that I have never been able to erase from my memory.

Chapter Six
FOXHOLES AND KOLIBAS

When the first rays of light began to filter through the eastern sky, we were thoroughly exhausted and looking for a recognizable marker to give us a clue as to our whereabouts. We made our camp deep in the forest to avoid the possibility of being seen by the German soldiers. The first task we needed to accomplish was digging the foxholes. We needed a place to rest and hide. The men finally used the heavy shovels they had carried for so many miles. They scooped up the earth and built a long trench, about four to five feet deep. It was to be our place of refuge from any bombs that might fall our way.

The adults knew what was important. Protection first; shelter next. As the grownups cleared an area to construct the shelters, they assigned the children the task of gathering firewood, berries, mushrooms, and anything that was edible. If we were going to survive, it had to be a team effort. Once again, we children were reminded not to wander off into the forest without an adult. By this time I was so terrified that not even the thought of chocolate could pry me away from Grandfather's protection. There were other instructions too. If we got separated or lost, we were to follow the nearby river in the opposite direction of the current. If we heard a whistling sound or a loud bang, we were to hit the ground, face down, and curl into a ball with our hands over our heads. Gosh, this was an awful lot for a little kid to remember.

The construction of our shelter was another team effort. One group of men cut down trees; the next group split trees into boards. It was helpful that one resourceful person had brought along an ax and another had brought a hand saw. And then there was Aunt Justina and her sewing machine! The children did their part and gathered ferns and leafy branches and placed them in a huge pile. Finally, the construction of the kolibas began.

A koliba is a shelter that looks much like a tepee. First, you place some boards on the ground, preferably on an incline. You do this so when the rains come, the water runs downhill under the boards, instead of flooding the inside of the koliba. Some kolibas are built into a hill, and some are built against a large tree. All are tied at the top with a rope. Wet mud is spread over the entire koliba, insulating and sealing it. Ferns and leafy branches are placed on top, and mud is spread once again over the entire area. Another layer of ferns and leaves are added on top while the mud is still wet, so as to create a camouflage with the rest of the forest. These structures provided a makeshift shelter that allowed us some protection from the elements.

There we were, in a forest somewhere between Slovakia and Poland. We were at least ten miles from our village, which was now occupied by the German army. Here, we had built our new community consisting of families, parents, children, grandparents, and neighbors. Each one of us had played a role. We had built our temporary home with sticks and mud and my aunt's sewing machine. A lot of good that machine did us.

Chapter Seven
EXPLODING BOMBS

When the kolibas were finished, the children gathered by the river and celebrated by scrubbing the mud and debris off our bodies. But our bathing and frolicking was soon interrupted by a thunderous noise above us. A tremendous explosion followed, hurling everyone briefly into the air and then crashing back to the ground. Dirt and debris came raining down on us.

As I got up from under the fallen debris, I was feeling dizzy and disoriented. I began searching frantically for my grandfather. He was running toward me and yelling for me to stay down on the ground. He scooped me up in his arms and headed for the foxholes. I remember thinking how smart we were to dig those foxholes first. The whistling, piercing sounds filled the air around us, and we were thankful for the trenches. When the bombs hit the ground, the earth around us shook violently.

Barricaded in our trenches, we huddled together, praying and crying. We began chanting the Lord's Prayer, Otçe Nash Iže Jesi, Na Nebesi (Our Father Who Art in Heaven), over and over again. God must have heard our prayers because all of a sudden, a hush fell over the forest. The noise had stopped, the planes had disappeared from the sky, and calmness once again prevailed. Wow! God must be pretty good, I thought. He plucked those planes out of the sky and threw them all away. Prayers are amazing! Boy, I am going to pray to God for everything . . . especially for chocolata.

Once the bombing ceased, people began to crawl out of the foxholes. I watched them emerge one by one and thought they appeared tattered and bewildered. Dirt covered all of us from head to toe.

But I was too afraid to move away from the foxholes, just in case God had missed some of those planes.

Chapter Eight
A TEMPORARY REFUGE

The planes and bombs seemed to be gone for now, and we got back to the daily task of survival. The elders took turns throughout the day and night, keeping watch for invaders slipping into our camp. It certainly paid off to be a kid at times like this. We were able to sleep through the night without any worries, while the elders had to keep a constant vigil.

Living outdoors brought its challenges. One day it was warm and the next, cold. Soon the rains came. As it poured, the rain softened the mud on the kolibas. Mother Nature was eroding our handiwork. Under the enormous weight of the soaked mud and greenery, the boards on several of the structures collapsed. Tragedy hit our enclave. A falling koliba crushed a mother and her two daughters. In the pouring rain, we mourned the first loss of our group members. We laid them to rest in a simple grave, marked by a wooden cross, close by in the woods.

As if the rain wasn't costly enough, the snow came early that autumn. As the ground began to freeze, we began to starve. The enticement of the food we left behind in the village consumed our thoughts. Some members of our group began making the long journey through the woods to sneak back to the village under the cover of night. Like thieves stalking their victims, they were forced to steal their own possessions. Grandfather was one of the first to make the trip, and he brought back news of the condition of the village. Soldiers now occupied our homes, and the destruction of our properties was readily apparent. The horses were dead, but the cows had been left in the pasture. During one of his journeys Grandpa was able to snag two cows and bring them back to our camp in the forest.

Many others in our group soon made the long trip back. Even Grandma and Aunt Justina made the journey. They would crawl for miles to be able to steal anything still edible in our village gardens. They used their bare hands to dig out abandoned potatoes. They grabbed fruit left unattended in the backyard orchards. They even retrieved some grain from a hidden storage bin. The fortunate ones returned, lugging burlap bags full of food on their backs. Some returned with frostbite, and some didn't return at all.

News came back that the German soldiers had captured other pilferers. They were interrogated, forced to dig trenches, and then shot at the site, falling into the trenches they had just finished digging. After hearing this news, Grandfather forbade everyone in our family from venturing back to the village. He, however, was exempt from this prohibition.

Chapter Nine
TRICKED

Early one morning, the roar of airplane engines in the distance awakened us. As the aircraft flew overhead, a shower of paper leaflets descended to the ground in a nearby clearing. What magic was this? We were eager to learn the message that was floating like manna from heaven. Cousin Michael carefully crept to the side of the clearing to retrieve a leaflet. The paper read: If you are a civilian, come out into the clearing and wave a white flag. We will not harm you! You will be protected.

The promise of protection and safety was a welcome and liberating proposal. The thought that someone in this horrible war would look out for us was enticing. Eagerly, grabbing anything that resembled the color white, we raced into the clearing, waving our crudely constructed flags. The adults got there first. The children gathered behind, working excitedly to find something white for their flags. I found a stick and tied an old handkerchief to it, waving it proudly as I skipped to join the others. The planes looped back, flying toward those already waving their white flags in the open space.

Suddenly, the sound of gunfire pierced the air, and bullets were flying everywhere. The white-flag celebration quickly shifted to hysteria, and people were running in all directions. As we retreated into the denser forest, the planes continued to pursue us. They were merciless. Diving in formation, they circled over us and then swooped down again. The whistling sounds of bullets, followed by violent explosions of the bombs, forced us deeper into the forest. Once again, I found myself running and screaming for Grandfather and Grandma. The white flag was discarded in the confusion. In the deafening noise, my cries were lost to all.

As I ran further into the woods, I tripped over a log on the forest floor. I lost my balance and started rolling down the side of a ravine. When I finally stopped, I was face down in mud, sopping wet, disoriented, and alone. Of course, I started to cry. When I tried to sit up, I realized that I couldn't see over the embankment above me. I sat there on the riverbank, isolated from my family, cold and wet and frightened. Yet somehow, the many rules and instructions came flooding into my mind. There was something about the current of the river. But was I to follow it or go the other way? This was so much for a kid to remember! I was bleeding from the scrapes, and I tried to wash the blood and dirt off my face and hands. The river water was so cold, and it stung my wounds. Then I thought about Grandfather and how he always tried to protect me. Suddenly, Grandfather's voice resonated clearly in my head: If you lose your way or become separated, just follow the river the opposite way of the current. I threw a stick into the water and watched it move, just as we had been instructed to do. As I saw the stick floating downstream, I turned and began running in the opposite direction. I was screaming for someone to help me and finally, Baba heard my cries. Coming to my rescue, she went to the edge of the ravine. The embankment was a bit lower there, and she was able to reach down and grab my hands, pulling me up to safety. I clung to her for a long time, just sobbing my heart out.

From that day forward, whether leaflets were descending from the sky or found on the ground, we would never trust their messages again. Trust was a luxury disappearing from our lives.

Chapter Ten
GRANDFATHER'S INTUITION

Despite the horrors of our current situation, Grandfather decided he must try to return to our village once again.

And this time he was caught.

He was discovered by the occupying Germans and thrown into the village jail. As luck would have it, an unknown partisan had killed a German soldier the previous morning. A partisan was an armed civilian, a guerrilla fighter, working against the occupying Nazi forces. Using an interpreter who could speak Slovak, the Nazis interrogated Grandpa and accused him of being the partisan who had killed their comrade.

Grandfather begged and pleaded with them, assuring them that he was not a partisan but simply an unarmed old man. He explained that the only reason he had returned was to find food for his starving family. He proceeded to name everyone in the family, including his infant grandson and his motherless and fatherless five-year-old granddaughter. Despite his desperate pleading, the soldiers turned a deaf ear.

These angry soldiers were not the same officers who first occupied the village and helped us with our escape. This time, Grandpa did not reveal his knowledge of the German language. Something inside, a sixth sense perhaps, alerted him to keep silent. After eavesdropping on their German conversation, he realized his fate. They were going to interrogate him further and then execute him at dawn, the same time that their comrade had died. He knew he must escape; there was no other alternative.

Sitting in our small, village one-cell jail, Grandfather channeled all of his thoughts and energies into a plan to get out before the morning sun filtered through the windows. He watched the guard dozing off, bobbing his head back and forth. Each minute seemed like an eternity. He began working around the window, chipping away some loose concrete. Fortunately for Grandfather, the building had been damaged during the bombing and was not structurally sound. After many hours, he managed to pry open a corner of the windowsill. He was fearful that the guard would awaken at any moment. He pushed and he pulled; finally, something moved. He loosened the frame enough to partially open the window, all while keeping one eye on the sleeping guard.

Just before dawn, Grandfather made the sign of the cross, took a deep breath, threw himself through that window, and crashed to the ground. The guard, no doubt startled awake, began shouting, "Halt! Halt!" The other guards came running and began shooting their guns through the open space where the window once stood. Grandfather never looked back. He kept running until he collapsed near the camp, where the rest of the villagers were anxiously awaiting his return.

That same night, the Germans captured two others from a neighboring village—an old grandfather with only one arm and a young boy. They, too, were accused of being partisans. Not as fortunate as Grandfather, they were shot and killed. After that, one other man was caught. He begged his captor to spare him because he had many children to feed. The soldier took pity on him, told him quietly that he should run for the woods and that he would be aiming his gun over the man's head. Thus, his life was spared.

After that night, there would be no returning to the village. We were forced to hunt for whatever food remained in the forest. We spent countless hours searching for mushrooms, berries, nuts, and other plants that could be boiled in water and eaten as soup. We made tea from wild rose buds. Yes, we learned the skills of survival very quickly, but food was always on our minds.

*My father, Nicolaj Hoç during his service
in the Czechoslovakian army.*

Chapter Eleven
A HANDSOME STRANGER

One morning as we went about our daily routine in the forest, a man approached our camp. I was peering from behind a tree and spotted him talking to Grandma and Grandfather. His uniform was different from the ones worn by my chocolate benefactors. It was green with ribbons on the arm, but there was no shiny helmet, and I didn't see a rifle hanging over his arm. He handed Grandma a bundle wrapped in brown paper, and then he turned and caught a glimpse of me.

As I ducked behind the tree, he walked toward me. Why was I shy and bashful about this soldier and not the others? Taking off his strange hat, which resembled the paper boats we made back in the village, he exposed a head of thick, wavy black hair. He smiled at me. I thought he was very handsome and I liked his big white teeth. I began hoping that he too would bring me chocolata.

"Marya?" he said. He seemed to know my name. I nodded my head. He extended his hand to me and said, "I am your father."

I didn't know quite what to do or say. To me, my mother and father were my grandparents. They were the only parents I knew. As a young child of four, I had been told that my mother was in a far-off land called America. For me, Mother was an abstract person whom I did not know. My life was complete with both a mother and a father figure in my grandparents, so this man's information didn't register at first. This was way too confusing for me. Grandma and Grandfather did not argue with him; they seemed to agree with his representation. They didn't even seem surprised. Why was I the only one feeling confused? I actually couldn't find any words to say to him, and I felt overwhelmed with emotions that I didn't understand. When I was able to think again, I noticed that he had brought bread in the brown package, as well as shoes for Grandma and me. But where had he come from, this soldier in the woods? And how come I didn't know anything about him?

My father's name was Nikolaĵ Hoć. He towered over me at five foot nine and had dark eyes and broad shoulders. I thought he was the most handsome man I had ever seen—besides my grandfather, that is. I discovered that he lived in the village called Habura, which was right next to ours. Imagine! I had a father I didn't know existed. As I learned later on, my mother had left for America in April 1939, when I was just four months old. At that time my father was off fighting with the Czechoslovakian army against the Nazis. When my mom left, she intended for me to follow soon after with my father, but then the war intervened, and I was destined to remain with Grandfather and Grandmother. I never questioned their role as my parents. I simply loved them with all of my heart.

While I knew nothing about my father, he knew about me, and he had kept track of where I was. News of our plight reached him while he was fighting, not far from our encampment. He came bringing nourishment and hope for the oncoming winter. He knew it would be tough for children to survive the cold in the woods, so he brought with him directions for a safe place where I could stay during the winter months. It was a home in Poland where his brother-in-law's relatives lived. He made the arrangements and said I would be leaving the forest soon.

Then he left as quickly as he had appeared.

It was a caring and heroic gesture for my father to bring us food, along with the shoes that I so desperately needed. He had crossed enemy lines to reach us, and he could have been killed. Later in my life, that bread and his efforts became meaningful not only for my body but also for my soul. But for now, in the midst of war and displacement, Grandma took charge of the bread. She rationed it to all the members of our camp community. And I felt proud because I was the reason we ate that night.

Chapter Twelve
UNWELCOME GUESTS

It was a small group that walked our way to Poland to stay with my father's relatives for the winter. Auntie Ava, Aunt Justina, baby Andrej, and I were hopeful and a little excited to be leaving the cold forest. I also was eager to meet new family members that I had never even known existed. However, when we arrived, the greeting we received was less than cordial. These new and distant relatives resented our intrusion. After all, they barely had enough food for their own family, so we were just an added burden. But then my father's sister-in-law Katrena spotted the two cows we brought with us, and her disposition suddenly changed. She visibly gulped—it must have been a long time since they had enjoyed fresh milk.

We were ushered to the barn, which had just become home to two other families—fifteen people in total. Among them were my father's two sisters and other relatives I did not know. The barn was cramped and damp. But the worst problem of all was that the barn was bug-infested. Just a few days before our arrival, there had been other inhabitants in the barn—Russian soldiers passing through. They left behind an assortment of varmints they had collected on their journey, including fleas and lice. We slept on the dirt floor that was covered with infested straw. We scratched ourselves until our skin bled. The fleas were like soldiers, waging war all winter and winning the attack on us.

One day, Russian army trucks came through the town, and each family member was given a voucher. We were allowed to walk to the nearby town, and everyone in our group could use the voucher to get rations of food and clothing. We now had something to contribute to the cranky in-laws' household. They stocked their coffers, taking charge of all of the rations. And with some food in the cupboards, all spirits rose just a bit.

We continued to exist in this unfriendly environment during the long winter months. We kept ourselves occupied by rolling in the snow, building forts, and having snowball fights. It was better than dodging bullets and bombs and at times, I almost felt carefree.

Then, as the signs of spring began to appear and the weather was warmer, the children were allowed to congregate on the front porch. One evening as dusk was taking hold, we were lying on the porch floor, hands behind our heads, listening to the peaceful chirping of the crickets. Staring at the darkening sky, I spotted the first star. This was a great achievement in our nightly entertainment, and it entitled me to a wish. "I wish I may, I wish I might, have this wish I wish tonight." My wish was, of course, the same as every other: "Please God, let this war be over so we can go home."

The quiet, the unrelenting crickets, and the sheer power of the dark sky suddenly got to me, and my usual strength of spirit simply dissolved. Crying, I regressed into my childish self. "I want to go home! I want to go home. Why do we have a war?" I wailed.

With this one question, I had broken through the cocoon of our survival. Before this, we had never even thought about why there was a war going on. We thought only about those things necessary for survival and just did what we had to do. Now, one of the youngest of the group had opened up the hearts and minds of the others—a group of disheveled and hungry kids, sitting in the middle of someone else's war.

The discussion was contagious. We started talking about what was happening in the village and which of our neighbors would never be seen again. Previously, any deep thinking had been pushed back by the needs of the moment. But now, all of the traumas that we had been through and all of those feelings we had bottled up inside were spewed out among us. It was more than I could take. In my young mind I knew it would have been better if I had never disturbed the cricket performance by asking that first question "Why?"

Chapter Thirteen
DANCING AGAIN

The days were getting longer and the cold was a little less bitter when the Polish lady named Katrena visited us in the barn. She told us it was time for us to leave because she could not feed us anymore. There were no more rations coming from the Russians. There were no more hikes to the village lugging home the sacks of food which Katrena would guard in her kitchen. Each family member had been allowed one ration of food and old clothing. Baby Andrej and I were a bonus—we counted for a full ration, but we were so little that we only needed part of the food. The rest of it was left for the others as payment for our lodging. But now that the rations were done, it was time to go back to the forest. We left the cows behind as payment for our keep, gathered our things, and said our good-byes. Hand in hand, we headed southwest—the two aunts, baby Andrej, and I—walking back to Czechoslovakia and our home in the forest.

Grandfather was very excited to see us, even though we were covered with flea bites. The forest life was much bleaker than when we had left. Some of the villagers went away, searching for shelter and food. The remaining villagers were thin and worn from the ravages of a bitter, starving winter. Grandma was one of the worst off. She was sick, and Grandpa was deeply concerned. Not long after we came back to the forest, Grandpa went looking for someone who could help Grandma with her horrible headaches. People were living everywhere in the forest. Walking in any direction, you could find others encamped on the sides of hills, with camouflage covering their makeshift shelters. But Grandpa could not find any medicine among the people scattered in the forest. Instead, he used the forest to treat Grandma's poor health. He cut the bark from a birch tree and had Grandma chew on it. He also found a neighbor who made alcohol from the forest wood. It was all he could find, and Grandma gulped the bitter drink, hoping to numb the pain.

As the days grew warmer, buds began to appear on trees, and soon color began entering our dreary existence. The sun felt good as it warmed our weary bones. The sound of gunfire and various explosions could barely be heard in the distance.

On one afternoon, I was leaning against a hill, looking up through a maze of lacy green leaves, and watching the sun filter through them. The sunlight created patterns and shapes on the ground, giving the appearance of couples dancing, having a wonderful time at a royal ball. I was lost in a daydream of a fantasy castle, thinking of how beautiful it all was. I wanted to stay this way forever.

However, I was jarred from my reverie by someone yelling, "The war is over! The war is over!" The messenger was running in circles, looking like a crazy person and shouting the same thing over and over again. But we all still heard the guns in the distance, and we remembered the flyers. We were not going to be duped again.

"A treaty was signed to end the war!" the crazy man shouted.

Some insisted that the distant sound of guns meant that the enemy was retreating. Could this possibly be true? We were afraid to believe anything good. Our dreams and hopes had been abandoned months ago. Then, as he continued shouting about the treaty, others joined him with the same story. People began to come out of hiding; they appeared out of the backdrop of the forest, looking like the forest itself, dirty and frail.

People began congregating, coming from every direction. The stories were all the same, and we began to allow ourselves to believe that the end of the war was actually a possibility. At first, the news was more of a trickle laced with skepticism, but the message picked up momentum, which turned to numbed, tentative belief. Even though we were weary and hungry, the stunned, quiet mood erupted into frenzied celebration. At last I could dance! And dance I did. Right there in the middle of the hugging and the kissing, I danced!

Everyone cheered me on. "Dance, Marya, dance!"

"The war is over! The war is over! Thank God, the war is finally over!"

Chapter Fourteen

RETURNING HOME

Gathering the tools and our few meager belongings, our exodus from the forest began. The journey home was decidedly easier than when we left. There were children skipping along without caution, playing tag and leapfrog. The grownups chatted away and hoped that they had something to come home to. Many of our possessions were hidden in the forest, with plans to go back for them later when we had a cart and a horse to pull it. Of course, Aunt Justina's sewing machine was most carefully hidden and later brought back to our home. And it actually did a lot of good because it raised our spirits to have some new clean clothing to wear after all that time of living in mud and dirt.

These folks were simple, hardworking, God-fearing people. All they really longed for was a roof over their heads, food for their families, and a peaceful existence. On that walk through the forest, many of them had a vision of the comforts of home that would be awaiting them. Nothing could have prepared them for the nightmare of pain and devastation that greeted them on their return.

The village was deserted, and it had an eerie and lonely feeling about it. We spotted the church on top of the hill overlooking the village. As we came closer, we saw the scars of destruction everywhere. Broken concrete littered the streets and every home appeared to be in a stage of demolition. As we pushed our way closer, the devastation became more evident. Spotting our home in the distance, I began jumping up and down.

"Home, home! Grandma and Grandpa, I see our home!" I shouted.

Breaking away from the group, I ran alone to reach my beloved home. The family members screamed after me to stop and wait for them. Disregarding their pleadings, I continued running until I reached our backyard. The fence was twisted and broken in places. The gate hung by a wire, swaying back and forth in the breeze. Once I got through the entryway, I ran at the speed of light to hug and kiss the walls of our home. In all the excitement, I paid little attention to the broken walls and crumbling concrete. As I ran gleefully along the tattered walkway, I suddenly felt excruciating pain in my right foot. Looking down, I noticed my little toe was caught in the broken concrete protruding from the house. Staring in disbelief at the blood gushing from my dangling toe, I was temporarily immobilized and in shock.

When I realized what had happened, I let out a blood-curdling scream. It brought everyone sprinting toward me. Grandma gently scooped me up when she glimpsed the blood along with the dangling toe. She sat down among the broken concrete shards and rocked me back and forth, trying to comfort me. She instructed my aunts to tear pieces of cloth from her long skirt and to bring water from the well. She proceeded to wash the blood off and place cold rags on my forehead. I finally fell asleep from sheer exhaustion.

When I awoke, the sun was setting behind the hills to the west. My foot was throbbing, and stepping down on it was just too painful. It was difficult for Grandma to find dressings for my wound among the ruins. But she was always resourceful and continued to rip scraps off her clothing to wrap around my toe. I was squirming in pain as Grandma attempted to soothe and console me. Was this to be the last wound of the war?

Back row (L–R) My mother, Aunt Sophie; Front row (L–R) Aunt Justina,
Grandfather, Grandmother, Aunt Jevka

Chapter Fifteen
THE SPOILS OF WAR

Now we were back home and waiting for life to return to normal. As I lay on a makeshift bed, nursing my foot, the adults worked on repairing our homes and surrounding lands. However, returning to the fields after the war introduced new dangers. Farmers were injured, and some were even killed while tilling the soil. This happened when they accidentally unearthed grenades not detonated during the long battles of the war. In addition, livestock was absent from the farms, and this made providing food an even bigger problem. Although the war was over, life had not become easy for the families in our village.

Grandfather and Grandma devoted all their attention to getting our house into livable condition again. We all slept in one room, which had a partial roof over it. The rest of the house was exposed to the elements. All the windows were blown out, and the walls were crumbling. This, however, was still home. When she wasn't working on our property, Grandma was busy nursing my foot back to health. She boiled well water, and when it cooled, she would wash the infected area of my toe. Then she applied a poultice made from a weed growing in the yard. I think the weed was called lišhaj. Finally, she would wrap the wound with a clean cloth. Despite her careful ministering, my foot became red and swollen and developed an abscess. When I finally began walking, I would shift the majority of my weight on to my left foot, skipping around out of fear of further injuring my right foot.

The kitchen area of our makeshift home featured a large oven constructed out of stone and clay. I could crawl on top of it to warm myself when it wasn't in use. I was sitting on top, feeling sorry for myself, when someone yelled out, "We have a visitor!" I quickly gave up my comfortable, warm spot on the oven to see who had come to visit. There were few visitors in those days, with everyone rebuilding their homes and putting the pieces of their lives back together. In the excitement, I forgot about my injured foot and jumped off from the top of the oven. And I did that with just enough pressure to break the abscess upon impact with the floor, releasing the poison. What a horrible sight. It felt as if my foot had exploded.

I was screaming, "My foot came off!" But Grandma assured me that now, at last, I was on my way to permanent healing. Although I still bear the scar on my right toe and am missing a toenail on the next one, I am amazed to this day at my Grandmother's resourcefulness and wisdom in the art of healing. The visitor turned out to be a postman delivering a letter from America.

One day during my confinement, while the foot was still healing, I sat on a bench that my Grandfather had nailed together out of scrap wood. I noticed four men and Grandpa walking across Uncle Stefan's yard toward our home. The four men were dressed in uniforms I didn't recognize. They spoke a foreign language to Grandpa, and he spoke in their tongue also. It was English. I discovered that Grandfather had spent many years working in the West Virginia coal mines before returning to Czechoslovakia. He had married Grandma in Elkhorn, West Virginia, and she had given birth to six children in the United States. Years later, they returned to their native country because Grandma was unhappy in West Virginia.

Grandpa introduced the smiling soldiers to me, and I smiled back. (Yes, of course I was hoping for a chocolata, although none came.) He told me that they were from America. My eyes lit up like a Christmas tree. I immediately asked if they knew my mother. The soldiers looked at me with sad eyes and shook their heads. I was very disappointed.

I thought everyone knew one another in America. After all, we knew everyone in our village! Grandpa called to Grandma and my aunts to come out and meet the Americans. The women brought out whatever food we had, sharing it with the soldiers. Grandpa wrote a letter to my mother, stating that we were alive and doing our best to put our lives back together again. He asked the soldiers if they could deliver it to my mother. They agreed to do so, thanked my family for the hospitality, and left after patting me on the head and waving good-bye.

We later learned that my mother did receive the letter Grandpa had written. However, she was already aware of our survival because she had contacted the Red Cross.

For my Grandparents, reality was setting in. They knew they were aging, and there was so much work to do to restore the village and our home. They were weary, and caring for a young granddaughter was becoming difficult for both of them. When the war ended I had been told that I would be leaving for America with my father as soon as the paperwork was completed. It was an exciting idea at first, finally meeting this mysterious mother. But nothing seemed to happen for quite a long time. Next, it was decided that I would leave for America with my Uncle Andy's wife, Aunt Sophie, as soon as all the papers were in order and passports received. I questioned what happened to my father and why the change of plans, but I never received an answer that I understood. Soon, Aunt Sophie received her passport and was ready to make the voyage to America. I, however, continued to wait for my passport. The disappointment made me inconsolable. I kept wailing, "I'll never get to see my mother!"

Little did I know that all this time there was another battle going on. This battle was taking place in the courts, and it concerned my custody. I was told that my father would not sign the documents permitting me to leave the country. I did not understand. Again, I questioned my grandfather. "Grandfather, why doesn't he want to sign the papers for me to meet my mother?" My grandfather was trying to cushion the blow of the unkindness of my father's refusal when he told me an unbelievable truth. "Your mother has remarried in America," he said.

I discovered that I had a whole new family in America. There was my mother, whom I had never met, a new father, and a little sister.

The fact was, I didn't want a new family. I liked the plan as it had been told to me years earlier—that I would travel to America with my father to meet my mother. I had only barely gotten to know my father, and now he was being replaced with an unknown person far away. Why did I have a new family? Why wasn't my father coming with me? If he wouldn't come, why wouldn't he sign the documents that would let me go? I had so many questions without answers. Divorce was not in our vocabulary. I didn't understand what it meant. Grandfather tried to explain that Mother and Father were no longer married to each other. In our world, the world of the Russian Orthodox Church, you were married for life. I remained confused for many years.

So, my tenuous future in America went back to the courts. Aunt Sophie was on her way to America, but I continued to wait.

Chapter Sixteen
A MATRIARCH'S PASSING

Grandma had been ill during the war with high blood pressure, and without medication, she suffered from tremendous headaches. Now, we were at home in our village, and although she had survived the brutal winter in the forest, she became gravely ill and suffered a stroke. Grandpa was beside himself, trying to find a doctor or medicine. Friends and relatives gathered in our home, lending whatever support they could, while I sat at Grandma's bedside keeping a vigil. I asked if I could sleep on the bench beside Grandma's bed. Reluctantly, she allowed me to remain there. I sat alone with my dying grandmother as life ebbed from her once strong, stout body.

Breathing became laborious for her. Grandpa and my aunts came in and out of the room frequently, trying to make her as comfortable as possible. In the early morning, the family gathered around the dying matriarch, wailing and crying hysterically. I was frightened, so I began crying along with them, afraid of being without my grandmother. Her breathing became more shallow, and she was desperately trying to speak. Grandpa and my aunts encouraged her to hang on, but she was too weak. All I could hear was a gurgling sound. We were witnessing Grandma's last breath, the death rattle, and the end of a courageous woman. As young as I was, I knew about death; I had seen it out in the forest during the war. But this was much more personal and painful.

The family left the room, sobbing. I stayed behind, watching my grandmother as she lay so still. "Why did you leave me, Grandma?" I asked her. Grandfather entered the room, closed Grandma's eyes, and led me away.

Neighborhood women came to prepare Grandmother's body for burial. As was the custom, her body lay in our home. Friends and relatives came to pay their respects. The funeral took place in the Russian Orthodox Church. My aunts had taken special care in dressing me properly. I was clad in Grandma's best creation with a ribbon in my hair. They didn't want to offend Grandma's meticulous taste. As we stood beside the wooden casket, constructed by friends and neighbors, I had flashbacks. I imagined Grandma packing picnic baskets as I tagged along to feed the workers tilling the soil in the fields. My pain was lessened by some poignant memories.

She was a disciplinarian in the strictest sense. Before the war, she had sewn an Easter outfit for me. On Good Friday, I was allowed to wear my dress, which was light green with a ruffle at the bottom and a white-and-green-striped pinafore on top. The pinafore tied into a bow in the back, and of course, included a matching bow for my hair! I went down to the meadow across the road, calling out for the twin girls who lived in the first house as you entered the village. I was skipping along, yelling for them to come out and play. As I came nearer, they began to taunt me about my outfit and the bow in my hair. They wore long braids, which I longed to possess.

They proceeded to attack me verbally. "Your mother left you! She didn't want you; that's why she left!"

I was stunned and began defending my mother. "She's going to send for me, and I'm going to America!" I retorted.

"No, she's not. No one wants you!" they said. At that moment, something inside of me exploded. I felt so much anger that I wanted to beat them to a pulp. They sensed the anger and took off running, with me in pursuit. As I was about to grab one of them, I tripped and fell, tearing and soiling my beautiful Easter dress. I knew I was in big trouble as they ran home, laughing.

I returned home, terrified as I stood in front of Grandma. She began to interrogate me. I had never lied to Grandma before, but I was just too scared to tell the truth. So I blurted out, "The twins from down the street called me names and pushed me." I thought that would be the end of it, but no, I was wrong. Grandma took me by the hand and marched me to the twins' house to confront them and their mother.

"Why did you push her?" she demanded.

They quipped back in unison, "We didn't push her. She just tripped and fell."

Grandma turned to me with fire in her eyes and demanded to know if that was true. I stuttered and finally said, "Well, they called me names, and they were taunting me. I started to run after them and almost caught one of them, but I tripped."

At that point, Grandma apologized to the mother, grabbed my hand, and marched me back to our house. After that I was black and blue in many places—the punishment for lying was severe. Grandma was angry about making a fool of herself when she confronted the mother and the twins. By Easter Sunday, my tarnished dress had been repaired. I sported a black eye, and marks from a willow-tree switch on my arms and legs. The black eye was from falling when I chased the twins. Boy, I never wanted to play with those girls again, and I avoided them like the plague.

As my thoughts continued to stray during the funeral, I recalled a horse that Grandmother was haggling over with a Jewish merchant who came through town trading horses for grain. The merchant stood next to the horse, and Grandpa, with his ever-present pipe in his mouth, stood next to the merchant. Grandma asked how many bags of grain he wanted for the horse. After negotiating back and forth, they finally agreed on a price. I followed Grandma when she went into the grain shed and began filling the designated amount of bags of grain. As she poured buckets of wheat into the bags, she paused and then switched to another method. Now, she poured oats over the wheat, and then topped it with wheat. It appeared that it was all wheat in the bag. When the merchant examined the grain, I looked at Grandma, about to say, "That's bad, Baba." She turned to face me and slapped my face so hard it left an imprint of her hand. Tears came streaming down my face, and I knew better than to utter what I was thinking. The exchange took place—the horse for the wheat. The merchant threw the grain into the wagon, jumped into his seat, and whipped the horses to go. Grandpa walked the horse to the barn and noticed that the horse was limping. Sure enough, Grandma had traded for a limping horse, and the merchant was given inferior grain. Grandma was furious and wanted to go after the merchant, but he was long gone by then. Poetic justice, I thought, smiling to myself through my tears.

When Grandma's funeral service was over, we walked over to the cemetery behind the church. The villagers had dug a grave there. A wooden cross was placed over the grave. Grandpa had ordered a cross made of granite with Grandma's name engraved on it. Unfortunately, it didn't arrive until months later. After the burial, the townsfolk came to our house to share the food that had been prepared by relatives and neighbors. I enjoyed the familiar smell of piroshkies until I realized that this time, my grandmother's loving hands had not prepared them. Everyone talked and reminisced about Grandma, and I left quietly to walk outside. It was such a beautiful, sunny day. I looked up at the blue sky and wondered, How could this be? How can anyone die, especially my grandmother, on such a beautiful sun-filled day? Feeling very alone, I kicked the stones in front of me, picked them up, and threw them at the trees. I felt confused and guilt-ridden for wanting to play when Grandma was dead. I walked around the front yard in a daze, not knowing what to do or where to go.

Grandfather came looking for me, wanting me to come in and have something to eat. Although I wasn't hungry, I went with Grandpa because somehow I knew we would both feel better if we were together.

Chapter Seventeen
LIFE WITHOUT GRANDMA

Life had taken a difficult turn with the death of my grandmother. Aunt Ava, her husband, and their son Andrej came to live with Grandpa, Aunt Justina, and me. I didn't get along with Aunt Ava's husband. He ordered me around, trying hard to be the authority figure who ruled my life. If I didn't listen to him and do what I was told, he would slap me. When I complained to everyone, they simply didn't believe me. I think the war left me with the ability to be more cunning in using my survival skills. I planned to stage a coup. Of course, I would carefully stage this so that my grandfather would be a witness to these disciplinary beatings. On one such occasion, I began antagonizing my tormentor by screwing up my face and sticking out my tongue when he ordered me around. I did this, knowing full well that Grandpa was within earshot. I kept my silence and that aggravated my aunt's husband even more. He came at me to give me a swift slap. I screamed. Grandpa caught him in the act. I've never seen Grandfather as angry as when he told the in-law he had better not put a hand on me again. Grandpa said that if I needed discipline, he would administer it. Needless to say, the uncle never raised a hand to me again. We coexisted in mutual hatred of one another. After Grandma's death, and this recent episode with the uncle, Grandfather's efforts to send me to America to live with my mother were heightened.

As I waited to go to America, my father would occasionally visit Grandfather and me in Ćertizne. They would pull two chairs close together and settle in for a bit. Grandfather would offer my father a small glass of Sljivovica, a kind of brandy made from plums. Then Grandfather would light his pipe and Father would start on his cigarette. My father respected and admired Grandfather—I could tell in the way they spoke to one another. They would share stories of the crops and livestock when I was around, but sometimes, when I was behind the corner or just creeping into the room, I could hear their hushed tones. Their voices always changed once they saw me.

Since it wasn't really spoken of during my childhood, it wasn't until many years later that I started stitching together the sketchy pieces of my family life. According to my calculations, my parents met in Çertizne. My father lived in the village of Habura, just west of Çertizne. The circumstances of their meeting are unknown, but I do know that my father asked Grandfather for my mother's hand in marriage. They were married in 1938, almost one year before my father was drafted to serve in the Czechoslovakian army.

I was born on January 4, 1939, two days after my mother's twentieth birthday. Four months later, my mother left for America. I was told that she left me with my father's family in Habura. I stayed there for only a couple of months. I ended up back with my mother's family in Çertizne. Many times I have questioned my mother about the reasons for my transferring between homes, but she insists she doesn't remember why—an answer that always surprises and disappoints me. The most important details in my own world hardly seem to have entered her mind.

When my mother left for America, she used her US passport, which was under her maiden name, Anna Šafran. Unlike my Czechoslovakian birth, she was born in Elkhorn, West Virginia. Thus, with a US passport, it was easy for her to leave Czechoslovakia and return to the United States. But why did she have to leave me behind?

My mother told me she had to stay in Bratislava on her way to America so she could change her documents to her married name, Anna Hoç. I have never seen such a passport in her possession. Instead, to this day, she cherishes and shows anyone who will examine it her worn and fragile passport in the name of Anna Śafran. I have always been filled with questions. At what point in time did the divorce occur? Where did it take place? I do not know the answers to these questions and likely never will.

At some point after the war, my father was told that my mother had remarried and wanted me to travel to America to live with her. The way I heard the story was that he was so angered by the news that he vowed to fight my mother to the bitter end. The problem was that the only thing he had left to fight her with was me. I was the pawn he could use to help him get even. He had found checkmate.

I was confused about so many things and sad that Grandmother was gone. I wondered where I really belonged and who would always take care of me and love me. To make matters worse, my Aunt Justina married Andreĵ Tahla, which became another loss for me. (And she took her sewing machine with her.) I felt close to Auntie Justina, and I didn't want her to leave our house. The wedding took place in the same church that held my Grandmother's funeral service. After the ceremony, Grandpa and Aunt Ava served a dinner in our home to honor the bride and groom. No music was allowed, as we were still in mourning over Grandma's death. After dinner, Aunt Justina and her husband left to live with his parents at the opposite end of the village. I was distraught over her departure and followed them to their new home. A wedding celebration was going on, and there was music and dancing, unlike the one at our house. There was cheering and toasting of the young couple. I wanted to stay all night. Of course, I was in trouble again, because I stayed too late. When I returned, after midnight, everyone was asleep, and the door was locked. We never locked our doors! I went to Aunt Jevka's window and tapped lightly so as not to wake Grandpa. She looked at me through the window and told me to be quiet, as Grandpa was furious with me. At that moment, Grandpa opened the door and ushered me inside. He grabbed a belt from a hook on the wall and said, "This is going to hurt me more than it will hurt you."

I pleaded with him in my sweetest voice, "Please, please, please, Grandpa! I don't want you to hurt yourself!"

He stopped his swinging arm in midair, his anger dissolving, and ordered me to go to bed. "I'll deal with you in the morning," he said in a much softer voice.

I went to bed, having lived through another day as a precocious child in post-war Czechoslovakia.

Chapter Eighteen
MY ONE-ROOM SCHOOLHOUSE

I started school at age six. The school was located in the center of the village. I had to cross over the bridge and follow the road along the top of the hill to reach the dilapidated building where the village children attended school. We sat in rows, according to our ages, and we had one teacher for the whole village for three years. I had great respect for Professor Ostapçhikanya, as she was a dedicated teacher. There was very little to work with, as far as materials and books, but she had a blackboard and chalk, and we had pencils and paper. Really, that was all that we needed. She had an innovative way of teaching, and we were a receptive audience. Later, the Russian government sent a professor from Moscow to teach us Russian. After the professor arrived, we spoke Russian for half the day, and the Slovak language for the other half.

The professor from Russia was a disappointment. His heart was simply not in teaching. It seemed to me that his priorities were more toward self-indulgence. As his students, we were made to plant his gardens during the school hours. We also had to tend to them until harvest time came along. The teachers and clergy were always treated well and held a place of prominence among the townspeople. We catered to their every need.

On Saturdays, we gathered in the classroom for catechism instructions. A priest would enter a room, and we would stand at attention until we were told to sit down. We were preparing for our First

Communion at age seven. We were the budding members of the Russian Orthodox Church's post-war First Communion class. "Write your sins down on paper," the priest said. This was the instruction given to us for our first lesson. We looked at the priest and then at one another, shrugged our shoulders, and began writing. I couldn't think of a sin that I'd committed. I listened to Grandma and Grandpa, but I didn't like the girl who lived next door. She'd scratch my face with her fingernails, but as mine were bitten off, I couldn't claw back. She had braids that I longed to have, so my choice of retaliation was to yank her braids, in the hope of separating them from her head. That must be a sin, I thought. I wrote it down. I stuck my tongue out at my uncle. That's got to be a sin! I compiled a lot of sins in a short time. Unfortunately, it wasn't a very difficult assignment for me. After class, the instructions were to go outside, tear up the paper with our sins written on it, throw them to the wind, and sin no more.

We were busily shredding the papers and tossing them, but I was curious about the sins my classmates had written down. I began chasing after the torn paper bits to see if I could read any of the sinners' confessions. Eventually, I gave up attempting to catch the swirling pieces of confetti. It really was none of my business after all.

Lesson two in catechism was to make the sign of the Cross when passing in front of our church and to greet passers-by with, "God be with you." While this was a ritual performed without question, it seemed difficult for me to accept things at face value. We had two churches in the village; one was Protestant, and one was Russian Orthodox. I began to wonder if the neighboring Protestant church taught the same lessons to their student congregation.

My question to our priest was, "Father, I know that we make the sign of the Cross when we pass in front of our church, but do we also make the sign when we pass by the Protestant church?"

The priest seemed a bit confused. No doubt, he was ready to deliver me to the Protestants. As he was deep in thought, he hummed a bit and then proceeded to answer my question by giving the class a little assignment. We were instructed to carefully observe members of the Protestant church as they passed our own church to see if they made the sign of the Cross in front of it. If not, then we didn't have to make the holy sign in front of their church. It was a clever way to avoid my question, which I felt was never answered.

Six weeks of instruction in our faith passed quickly, and we were to make our First Communion the following Sunday. Our household was busy cooking and baking for the big celebration following the ceremony. Sugar was in short supply, but sweetness was everywhere for this special occasion. Temptation once again accosted me. I managed to sneak a lick of frosting from one of the tarts. I was horror-stricken as I remembered we weren't supposed to eat anything before receiving Communion. I spent the next several hours spitting out and washing my mouth of the forbidden fruit, while keeping a watchful eye that no one was looking. I reasoned that since I hadn't swallowed the sweet concoction, I had not really succumbed to the temptation. I proceeded to make my First Communion along with my classmates.

We stood in the front row of our church while participating in the ceremonial Mass, all of us dressed in our finest attire. I was clad in a dress that my mother had sent from America for the occasion. However, my beautiful dress already had a history.

Two weeks before, our professor's wife had approached me to ask about my pretty dress from America, wondering if I would let her daughter borrow it for her First Communion, which was a week before mine. I was stunned and unable to speak for a few seconds. How can she be so bold and insensitive? I thought. But I finally croaked out "Okay," very disappointedly. I felt as though I had no choice but to say yes. After all, she was my teacher's wife. She was very excited and promised to take extra good care of the dress and veil. My aunts were not happy that I agreed to loan my dress. I wasn't happy either when I saw my beautiful dress marching down the aisle past me. The communicants were lined up in the front row and all were handed a lit candle while the bishop and priest conducted the ceremony. The professor's daughter tilted her head to the right while holding the lit candle in her right hand. My veil caught on fire while the congregation looked on, horrified. Her mother ran down the aisle, reaching for the burning veil, and extinguishing it by slapping it around in her hands. The daughter was stunned, obviously not realizing what was happening. The fire was put out successfully, and the ceremony continued. But all I could think about was that my beautiful dress from America was spoiled before I even got to wear it.

The dress, however, was patched up, and I was able to participate in my own First Communion the following week. I admit, though, that the excitement of that day just never felt the same to me because I knew my special dress was damaged. Once the ceremony ended, we all went home to enjoy the banquet prepared by my aunts. Our cousins joined us, and we were happy. Of course, all the buzz continued to be about my burned veil. I gorged myself with the sweets until I became queasy. All in all, it was a wonderful ending for my First Communion.

Our Russian Orthodox Church in Çertizne

My father, Nicolaj Hoç in his prime

Chapter Nineteen
COMING TO AMERICA

Eventually, we won another battle. I received word that I could travel to America. I don't know what made my father change his mind, but I began preparing for the journey of a lifetime. I fantasized about my reunion with my mother. I imagined us running toward one another and embracing, hugging, kissing, and crying tears of joy. On a beautiful Sunday afternoon in August 1949, I carefully packed my little suitcase with a few items—one change of underwear, a pair of white socks, and a petit point piece that my Russian teacher's wife gave to me. (Of course, in exchange, she asked me to send her colored threads once I arrived in the United States.) My aunts checked the contents of the suitcase. Satisfied with the items I had chosen to take, they gently closed it. I was now ready to walk to the bus stop and ride off to a new life.

I felt so proud and happy, carrying my suitcase, walking next to Grandpa and my two aunts, plus some neighbors and cousins. They bid me a safe journey, asking only that I didn't forget them. I promised I wouldn't. The bus arrived, and I kissed my aunts good-bye. I jumped into the bus along with Grandpa and waved good-bye to everyone. I noticed that my aunts, dressed in green attire, dabbed the tears away from their eyes with white embroidered handkerchiefs. I'm not sure if I was witnessing tears of sadness or happiness that I was leaving. I would tease them about it many years later. The bus began to roll off, and everyone waved at us, while Grandpa and I waved back. I took my last look at our house as we passed by. I was looking forward to the journey ahead.

The next bus stop was in Habura, where my father resided. He lived there with his new wife in his family home, which was attached to a small grocery and candy shop. He was waiting at the bus stop. When the door opened, he jumped in, paid the conductor, and then sat next to Grandpa. They chatted about how I would like America, and Grandpa assured him that my life would be better there. As I mentioned before, Grandpa was an honorable man. He got along with most individuals, including my father. It was Grandma who didn't like my father and who had encouraged my mother to leave for America.

Our final bus stop was Medzilaborce. Here we were to board a train for our next destination, which was Prague. My father wanted to travel with us to Prague. Grandpa insisted that it wasn't necessary for him to go, as we had appointments set up at the American embassy. Grandpa was cautious while dealing with my father, as he didn't want anything to go wrong before my departure. We had some free time before boarding the train, so Grandpa suggested to my father that we should stop at the pub and get a drink. My father agreed wholeheartedly. After several drinks, he became melancholy, wanting to accompany us to Prague. Grandpa ordered him another drink, a calculated maneuver on his part. After that drink, Grandpa paid the bus driver for the return fare and sent my father back home. Luckily for us, my father took his leave peacefully.

It was finally time for us to board our train. The train whistle blew as the conductor yelled, "All aboard!" The train began to move, slowly picking up speed. I watched the trees and fields pass by, and I was mesmerized by the beautiful sunset. The steady thumping of the wheels made me feel drowsy. I reached in my sweater pocket for my rosary. It was made of chartreuse crystal beads and it had been presented to me at my First Communion. With the beads in my little fingers, I began saying my nightly prayers. I fell asleep somewhere between the "Our Father" and the "Hail Mary," and the rosary slipped from my hand.

I was awakened when the train came to a sudden stop. It was bright and sunny outside, and Grandpa announced that we were in Prague. Because we still had paperwork to complete for my passport, we had plans to stay with relatives who lived in an apartment in town. We went to the consulate, and I had my picture taken while Grandpa answered all the questions the consulate people asked. They told us to return the following day to sign the passport, finalizing it with a seal on the document. I would then be ready to leave for America.

Here I was, a country bumpkin, visiting my big-city cousins. I was as much of a curiosity to them as they were to me. They spoke the Czech language and I spoke Slovak, Ukrainian, and Russian—quite a combination. Somehow, between all four languages, we connected. At one point, I needed to use the bathroom facility, and they had to show me how to turn on the faucet. As they turned it on, I quickly jumped and placed my hands under the sink to catch the flow of water. They began laughing uncontrollably. They didn't know I had no knowledge of running water, sinks, or toilet bowls. Back home on the farm, we had a well and an outhouse. Next, they took me to my first movie. I can't recall what the film was about, but I felt like I was in the land of Oz. Everything new seemed strange to me. My cousins were angels for putting up with me, a country mouse.

I was to leave for America the next day. I kept thanking my cousins for their hospitality and patience. To celebrate our last day in Prague, Grandfather thought we should do some sightseeing. We started out by having lunch at a café in the middle of town. Then we crossed the St. Charles Bridge and strolled down to Old Town to look into the local shops. Grandpa spotted me eyeing a brooch displayed in a jewelry shop window. He took me by the hand and led me inside, asking the salesperson if he could see the purple flowered brooch in the window. He then asked me if I liked it.

"Oh, Grandpa, it's beautiful!" I exclaimed.

"A souvenir from Prague," he said as he purchased it for me. I thanked him and told him he shouldn't have bought me such a costly piece of jewelry. But I was so pleased that he did!

I began searching my sweater pockets for my rosary, but I couldn't find it. I was trying desperately to remember where I might have placed

My passport photo page in 1949

it. I recalled saying my prayers on the train and figured the rosary must have fallen between the seats. I was quite upset over the loss. But my dear grandfather kept assuring me that I could get another rosary and have it blessed by a priest in America.

The next morning, we bid good-bye to our relatives and walked to the bus station for the trip to the airport. I was excited and nervous at the same time.

"I can't wait until we're in the plane and finally going to America!" I said to Grandfather. "Aren't you excited, Grandpa?"

A sudden sadness came over his face as he looked down at me. "Marya," he said, "I'm not going to America with you."

I looked at him as if he had just slapped me in the face. "Grandpa, you are joking with me," I said in despair.

"No, Marya, I'm not joking with you."

"Why, Grandpa, why? I can't go by myself! I don't know the language, or where I'm supposed to go, or even what my mother looks like! Please, Grandpa, don't leave me!" I begged.

I was hysterical by the time we reached the airport. He tried to explain that he was too old to travel to America and that he wanted to be buried next to Grandmother in Ćertizne. By the time we reached the tarmac, passengers were already boarding the plane. I begged and cried louder and louder, causing quite a disturbance.

"No! I'm not going without you!" I yelled. "I want to stay with you!"

The stewardess walked toward us to escort me to the plane. I grabbed Grandfather's leg and wouldn't let go. I was crying so hard that I started shaking. I begged him again not to leave me. My poor grandpa wiped his face with a handkerchief and tried desperately to calm me down. The flight attendant didn't quite know what to do next. She knelt down on one knee, trying to explain that I had to go with her and take my seat on the plane. I wouldn't let go of Grandfather's leg, so she eventually had to pry me away from him. As she led me away, it felt as though my whole world was coming to an end. I kept turning back, looking at Grandpa. He kept assuring me that I would be fine; I'd have a better life.

I started up the stairs, still hoping he would change his mind and come with me. I turned back one more time. He was still standing by the fence, looking sad and forlorn, and wiping his face with his handkerchief. I went inside and sat in my seat by the window. I was still crying, and I pushed my face up to the glass so I could see him better. The stewardess buckled my seatbelt. The engine roared as the plane began to move. I craned my neck to get one last glance at the person who meant the world to me. I must have cried myself to sleep.

The next thing I recall was the stewardess waking me up as the plane was landing in London, England, the next stop on my journey to America. A passenger on the plane came to my seat and interpreted what the stewardess was instructing me to do. She led me off the plane with my little suitcase in my hand, toward a large terminal. I was handed to a lady named Anne Kelly, who had visited Ireland and was on her way home to Detroit, Michigan. When she was asked if she would take charge of me and deliver me to my mother at the airport in Detroit, she had readily agreed.

When I met her, she took me by the hand, and we headed to the bathroom to freshen up my tear-stained face. I looked up at Anne Kelly and couldn't stop staring at her. I thought she was the most beautiful lady I had ever seen. She reminded me of Snow White. Her hair was pitch-black, her skin was porcelain white, and she wore the reddest lipstick! That red lipstick made her teeth look as white as snow. I watched her every move. She smiled a lot. Her black hair was cut in a medium-length bob with straight bangs across her forehead. She led me to a toilet stall and stood guard outside the door. As I came out, she led me to the sink, where she washed and dried my face and hands with a paper towel. She also brushed my hair and placed the barrette back on my head. I kept staring at her and returning her smile, entranced. I trusted her instantly. We became friends and were both proficient in pointing—because of the language barrier, it was the best way to communicate. (We could've been referred to as the "Pointer Sisters.") We were not unlike the two stars in the Big Dipper, the ones that are in a direct line with the North Star.

Soon it was time to leave, and she guided me back on to the plane. Anne sat next to me and showed me pictures of buildings, flowers, and food. I was really enjoying my newfound friend. The trip across the Atlantic was long and tedious. It seemed like there was an endless stretch of water underneath us and few clouds in the sky. I couldn't differentiate between the ocean and the sky. When the sun finally set in the western sky, the stars began to appear. Darkness enveloped us, except for a few dim lights inside the plane. We fell asleep but were aroused from our slumber by a stewardess rustling things while moving down the aisle.

Passengers began discussing the approaching New York City skyline. Anne pointed to many large buildings, bridges, and a big lady with a crown on her head in the harbor. After we landed, she led me by the hand to the restroom to freshen up for our last stop before meeting my future. By this time, I was feeling quite confident and conducting myself with self-assurance. Indoor plumbing in the bathrooms no longer confused me.

Suddenly, there was a flurry of people surrounding us. Through an interpreter, I was told to sit on top of some suitcases. I was handed an apparatus (a telephone, I later learned) to place next to my ear. It made an annoying buzzing sound. Then a man coaxed me to say, "Hallo Amereeka." A flashbulb went off as my picture was taken. Apparently, someone in the public relations department of the airline company had told the press that a young girl was traveling alone to meet her mother for the first time. UPI picked up the story, and sent a photographer to take my photo. The headline read, "Slovak Girl Reunited with Her Mother after Ten Years."

Then Anne Kelly and I connected to our final flight, the short trip from New York City to Detroit, Michigan—my new home in America.

*My stepfather, Julian Bobak, during his service
in the US Army, and my mother*

Chapter Twenty
WHO AM I NOW?

Once in Detroit, Anne took me by the hand, and I continued to carry my little suitcase in my other hand. We descended the stairs toward a small group of people who appeared to be waiting for someone. Anne approached a woman and asked her for her name. The woman replied, "I am Anna Bobak. I think that is my daughter Marya." Anne let go of my hand. The woman came closer to me, bent down, and awkwardly gave me a brief hug. I didn't know what I had been expecting, but I somehow felt disappointed. Then I spotted my Aunt Sophie and ran to her, hugging and kissing her, relieved that I had found someone I knew and who allowed me to feel that I was in a safe harbor.

There had been no photos of my mother, only a description of her from Grandfather. I wasn't really sure what to expect, but the woman who said she was my mother was of average height, about five foot five. She was slender, with blonde hair done in a pompadour style, with deep waves on both sides that turned to a pageboy in back. She was dressed in a dark blue fitted dress. I thought she was nice-looking.

She introduced me to my stepfather and a three-year-old sister, who I thought resembled Shirley Temple. This new sibling had curly blonde hair, a pink ruffled dress, and black patent leather Mary Jane shoes. As I bent down to hug her, she hauled off and kicked me in the shin. She was immediately scolded by both parents.

I jumped to her defense. "Oh, that's okay. She didn't hurt me," I assured them. "She didn't mean it. She just doesn't know me."

I met my Uncle Andy, Mother's brother and Aunt Sophie's husband. At some point, my mother thanked Anne Kelly, and they exchanged addresses. I thanked Anne for taking care of me and told her I hoped I would see her again. Mother interpreted my little speech to her. Anne smiled and said, "Yes, I will come to visit you." Anne bid us good-bye and then walked away.

My homecoming was not what I had expected. When I look back, I can understand that my mother and I weren't able to bond in my formative years, when trust and closeness is established. Apparently, this had been a void in both of our lives. She was a stranger to me, and I was to her. I had a difficult time adjusting to a ready-made family. It wasn't what I dreamed and fantasized about during our time apart. The lack of warmth from my new family made my longing for my grandfather intensify. I wanted to go back to what was familiar.

The ride to my new home in the moving machine was quite thrilling. My stepfather's blue Plymouth provided my first ride in a car. Heading toward my new home in Dearborn, Michigan, I was mesmerized by all the street lights, as well as the flashing lights in different colors—red, yellow, and green. I asked a thousand questions: "Are these lights on all the time?" "Doesn't it get dark in America?" "Don't people sleep here?" "There are so many cars—where are they all going?"

We drove into a detached garage that I thought was the house. Then we entered a bigger house, and I was shown to my bedroom. My own bedroom! I couldn't believe I would have my own bedroom, my own bed. This was all too much to take in.

I finally went to bed, but as exhausted as I was, I couldn't sleep. I had been traveling for twenty-four hours, but my sleep patterns were messed up. I kept waking up and going to the window to look at the streetlights. I couldn't understand why somebody didn't turn them off. The time zone change played havoc with the patterns my body was accustomed to.

The next day, I asked my mother, "Doesn't it ever get dark in America? How can anyone sleep here?"

She answered, "Don't worry; you'll get used to it. We'll put some shades on the windows." In the meantime, there was lots of excitement with relatives, friends, and neighbors visiting and bringing gifts. I got so much attention as the new family member that it was no wonder my little sister, Rose, threw tantrums. She had been the center of attention until this stranger came into her world.

A few days later, a reporter from the Detroit Free Press called, wanting to interview me and my mother. Mother had taken me shopping for a new dress. Then she dropped me off at a beauty salon, instructing the beautician to give me a perm. And then she left me there, alone. The salon worker sat me down, placed my hair in rollers, and plugged me into a machine. I didn't know what they were doing to me. Besides that, I was becoming dehydrated, for it was a hot day in August. I kept motioning to the lady that I wanted a glass of water. She brought me a sandwich. I shook my head. "No! No!" In my own language, I was repeating, "Voda, voda," meaning water. I pretended to hold a glass, tilting my head back in an exaggerated way and drinking invisible liquid. She then uttered, "Oh, you want water?" I nodded my head "YES!"

She brought a glass of water, and I emptied it in seconds and asked for another and another—I drank three glasses, one after another. Of course, then the next lesson was learning to ask where the bathroom was. This language barrier was becoming too much for me, and I could feel a determination forming to learn English fast!

Finally, my mother came back, and I was unplugged from the machine. The rollers in my hair were unwound. It looked like a Brillo pad had been placed on my head, but I thought I was the cat's meow—truly all-American now. I was all spiffed up for the newspaper interview. I made it to the bathroom, my beauty experience complete.

The headline in the newspaper story read, "An American for Five Days; She Loves It." The photographer snapped the picture with my mother kissing my cheek, and I looked at the camera with a big smile. I became an instant celebrity—my fifteen minutes of fame. I had to smile until my face hurt and soon couldn't wait for it to be over. My mother, however, seemed to enjoy the attention. After the news article appeared, friends, neighbors, and even strangers came over bearing gifts, wanting to see the girl who travelled by herself from Czechoslovakia to be reunited with her mother.

All this attention did not sit well with my little sister Rosie. She was no doubt resenting this stranger coming into her domain. She had been the little princess and now she had to share her throne. She didn't find out that we were half-sisters until she was around thirteen years old, and she was devastated. She had no idea that we had different fathers. Our family just didn't bring up the subject.

Like any child, I was curious about my father and mother's relationship, especially why they were divorced. Now that I was with my mother in America, I tried to get some answers. The little I found out, though, was when my mother would scream at me while berating my father with such scorn that it made me shudder. It's very hurtful to hear disparaging remarks about one's parent, regardless of the circumstances. My mother blamed him for his drinking, womanizing, and other infractions. I was aware that my father enjoyed his drinks. I also knew that most men in the small villages back home sought refuge at the village pubs. There was little to do in the countryside for entertainment. When I asked my mother about the allegations and how she learned about them, she responded that people had written to her about him. And she said that is why she changed her mind about bringing him to America.

Here I was in America, and I had a fill-in for my missing father in my stepfather. This didn't work out as well as I had hoped. My stepfather wasn't exactly the take-charge type of individual. He would take the easy way out. My mother ruled the household. What she said or what she wanted done was indisputable.

My mother asked me what name I wanted to use in America. The question took me by surprise. I sputtered, "I don't really know, I haven't thought about it." I had been Marya Hoć for ten years, and I felt uneasy changing my name. As I pondered this, I came to the conclusion that it would simplify things if I used the same name as my new family. I became Mary Bobak.

By this benevolent gesture, I unwittingly created some problems later in life. Applying for a marriage license and social security card became a challenge. (My advice is to be careful what name you use, and have your name changed legally.) At the time, my parents just didn't realize the problems that would develop with my changing my name.

Soon after my arrival in America, the many cultural differences became apparent. I had grown up on a farm and now was thrown into city life. Food was different. It tasted bland and watery to me. I couldn't drink regular milk, only buttermilk or curdled sour milk. It was what I was used to, since we had no refrigeration on the farm. Mother thought I was being stubborn and defiant. She forced me to drink the milk. I gagged and threw it up, and severe punishment followed.

At age ten, I had my own opinion of America. I arrived here believing that the streets of America were paved with gold and that everyone was

Detroit News article

rich! The idea that people had to actually work to achieve the good life somehow was never an integral part of my teaching while growing up in Europe. We were prisoners of our own ignorance, unaware that hard work was necessary outside of our small village. What I did find different was the availability of opportunities for success. I would learn that while the streets were not paved with gold, there were avenues of golden opportunities. I was destined to learn not to value the price of a metal but to gain an appreciation for the creativity that existed in the absence of oppression. This I learned years later.

After the whirlwind of events in the first few weeks of my new life, we settled down to a daily routine. Mother called me to the kitchen, announcing, "I didn't say anything to you before, but now you will have to start helping out around the house." I was taken aback by the remark. I had every intention of helping. I just didn't know what I was supposed to do.

Chapter Twenty-One
NOW I AM MARY

Three weeks later, in September 1949, Mother walked me to school to register for fifth grade at Woodward Elementary School, just four blocks from our home. Someone in the office took me by the hand and I was ushered to a classroom, where I was introduced to a teacher and shown where to sit. I sat there for forty-five minutes, just listening but not understanding much of what was being said. I did understand when my name was mentioned, and my classmates turned their heads to look at me.

Mrs. Wilkie, our math teacher, spoke Ukrainian and was able to communicate with me in her classroom. She informed her class that the new student didn't speak English and told them to help me and direct me to my classes. At first, everyone wanted to help. Soon after, it got to be a tedious task, and I had to fend for myself. The worst part was the boredom I encountered. I sat in the classrooms hour after hour, not understanding a word.

Reality was setting in. I found myself in unfamiliar surroundings, trying to learn English, trying to fit in to a ready-made family, and trying to make new friends and attend school. I felt overwhelmed by the adjustments and demands. I was lonely and missed my grandfather and friends.

One day I started crying and said that I wanted to go back to live with my grandfather. I complained bitterly to Mother that I hated it in America. I didn't want to go to school. I wanted to go back to live with Grandpa.

She got angry and annoyed. "Now get this through your head. You can't go back; you're here to stay. You have to go to school and learn English, and that's the end of it. I don't want to hear about it again."

I hated the America I once longed for. "I hate school. I don't know what the teachers are talking about. I sit in class, not understanding anything. I'm bored to death. During recess, everyone is playing and running around. I stand alone, watching and not knowing what to do," I said.

Because I was miserable, I decided I would not go to school anymore. I left in the morning and took my lunch bag. Then I walked to the corner and hid behind a house until the other students passed. For the rest of the day, I sat next to a tree, playing some imaginary game or making a ring or bracelet from the grasses I would gather. I ate lunch from my brown bag and walked the streets until school let out. Then I walked home. I continued this charade until the school called my mother, asking why I wasn't attending school. Mother was dumbfounded and told them, "She leaves for school in the morning and comes back after school is out."

Well, when I got back from my pretend school that day, my mother was not happy. "Where have you been?" she demanded.

"I was in school," I lied.

"The principal called and wanted to know why you were absent," she retorted.

I knew the jig was up. I started to cry. "I told you that I hate it here. I want to go back to live with Grandpa," I sobbed.

"And I told you, you can't go back. Get that through your head," she replied.

The next morning, Mother marched me into the principal's office. She said I'd skipped school because I didn't like being there. The principal told my mother to speak English at home so I could learn it and assimilate more easily. I knew there was no way out but to try to accept and embrace this new culture that I presently hated.

Mr. Rhodes, the art teacher, would take me aside and coach me by holding an object, such as a pencil, and then make me repeat the

English word several times. After class, he would test me. Mrs. Wilkie, the Ukrainian teacher, would come in an hour before school to help me with math. At home, I would watch TV shows such as Howdy Doody and Kukla, Fran, and Ollie. These were my early educators, along with the teachers at Woodward Elementary School. I decided I would not speak my native tongue unless it was absolutely necessary. From this day forward, I thought, I will be an all-American girl.

As I progressed in the language department, I longed to be just like my classmates. I began to emulate them in dress, sports, and speech—though speech was a bit more difficult to imitate. I was assigned to Miss Pashke, a speech teacher. Once a week, I spent an hour with her, articulating words and sentences. There were other students with speech impediments, such as lisping, and some couldn't pronounce certain letters, so they were part of the speech class too.

Miss Pashke came to class smelling of chocolate! She evidently enjoyed a Hershey bar before our session. I would salivate throughout the hour over that chocolate, inhaling the aroma as she spoke.

I was beginning to believe that America would like me. My English was improving, communicating was easier, and I was excelling in sports. Baseball was my absolute love. I would organize kids from the neighborhood and play softball every chance I could. I was definitely a tomboy. In Europe, I had played soccer, rode horses, climbed trees, and run barefoot in the snow. In America, all sports intrigued me.

Our neighborhood in Dearborn was truly a melting pot of people from around the world. Next door on one side were the Palidores. Lena, the mother, communicated with warmth, although the language barrier was virtually impossible at first. Once I learned to speak English, however, we became friends. On the north side, our neighbors were the Czans. They spoke a form of Russian-Carpathian, which I believe is a dialect of Russian and Slavic mixture, spoken around the Carpathian Mountains region. There was Mrs. Mary Czan; her husband, Dimitri; and daughters, Mary Jane and Patsy. Patsy was the role model for the young girls in our neighborhood. She was attending Fordson High

School. She was a great dancer and taught us dance steps to the jitterbug. She spoke the Russian-Carpathian dialect along with her mom and dad. Mary Jane, a year younger than me, understood the language but had difficulty speaking it. I couldn't wait to grow up, go to dances, and be just like Patsy.

The Cloughs lived behind us. Carol Clough was part of our group. There was also Vicky, who lived with her aunt and uncle a few doors away. Together, we girls roamed the neighborhood as a benign gang, enjoying each other's company as we grew to become teenagers. Of course, my little sister Rosie always tagged along.

These were my first friends in America. I treasured their friendships then and will always be grateful to them, because they allowed me to feel like I belonged.

Once I learned the language, doors opened for me, and I felt more comfortable blending in with the rest of the student body. I joyfully participated in sports and planted a summer garden on land donated by the founder of the Ford Motor Company, Mr. Henry Ford. He wanted students to learn how to cultivate the land, so he encouraged us to raise vegetables to keep or sell for profit. It was exciting and fun, competing with friends to see who could raise the biggest crop. Unfortunately, it wasn't me. I had a taste of the city life and found that I didn't want to go back to the farm!

After a year, I was integrating and becoming completely Americanized. I continued with my plan to avoid speaking in my native tongue at home, unless it was absolutely necessary. Just as I was beginning to feel somewhat comfortable and looking forward to attending Fordson High School in a few years, Mother broke the news: we were going to move to Utica, Michigan.

We had to move because the factory where both of my parents worked was moving to Utica, but I was distraught over the move. I had made friends and had begun to feel at home with my surroundings. Now, I had to start all over again. I was beside myself. Why was this happening to me just as I was beginning to feel comfortable and confident? I didn't

Woodward School with Class 7-A1, sitting front and center

want to leave my friends or the teachers who had painstakingly taken the time to teach me English—Mrs. Wilkie, my wonderful math teacher, and Mr. Rhodes, the art teacher who encouraged me to draw and paint along with helping me with my speech. I especially loved my gym teacher, who taught me how to swim when I was so afraid of the water. She encouraged me to excel in all sports because she saw my potential and recognized my instinct for competitiveness. How could I say good-bye to all of those people? It was the end of seventh grade, and I just didn't want another change in my life.

Thus, it was an unhappy teenager who moved to Utica, Michigan, a farming community on the outskirts of Detroit. Utica was quite the rural area compared to Dearborn. It was an agricultural community and typical small-town USA. There were a few stores, a pharmacy, a shoe repair shop, a sweet shop, an A&W drive-in, a flower shop, a dry cleaners, and assorted restaurants.

Once again, I felt isolated and self-conscious while trying to adjust to the new location. The first thing on my self-appointed agenda was to rid myself of my European accent. This turned out to be no easy task. Often, it seems that the harder you try, the more the accent becomes apparent. I was frustrating myself with my efforts, but I kept vowing to try harder. I still slip up on those pesky Rs and Ws. In my native tongue, you roll the Rs, and there is no sound for "th." W is not in the vernacular because we substitute the letter V for W. I would sit in front of the mirror enunciating each syllable of every word that contained those letters. I would do it over and over again. My classmates thought my accent was charming; I didn't. I tried so hard to eliminate it. I would get furious with myself when I slipped up and the accent became apparent. I didn't want that marginalized feeling. I wanted to fit in.

Now, I can empathize with foreign students and their families who come to this country. The parents want to keep their traditions and beliefs. Students are torn in both directions. They want to fit in with their peers while respecting their parents, who want desperately to hang on to their culture. Many times, there is a war of cultures in those families.

I always wanted to assimilate to the culture where I was living. Following the old adage, "When in Rome, do as the Romans do," I fought to fit in. That didn't always sit well with my parents. They too clung to the traditions and mores of the old country. I fought back; I wanted to be the All-American Girl. I wanted to be "Thoroughly Modern Mary."

Chapter Twenty-Two
UNEXPECTED TREASURES

While life seemed frenzied and unpredictable, I now realize that this is a normal state of being for any teenager, with the inherent perplexities common to all adolescents.

On the first day of high school, I was dressed in my new clothes, which I'd purchased from my babysitting money. My new wardrobe consisted primarily of fall and winter sweaters, skirts, and various accessories. My classmates and I just had to wear the newly purchased clothes, even though the weather dictated lighter attire. As we entered the classrooms, the heat inside was stifling. We couldn't wait to get back home and peel off the sweaty woolen clothes. But we all agreed that first impression was important. From that day forward, the standard dress was more casual. I joined the fashion dictates in looking like everyone else and feeling more comfortable. I decided that this was the simplest way to fit in.

I enjoyed participating in the physical education programs and tried every sport available—track, softball, volleyball, basketball—and I even broke a few records in track! These physical activities provided an outlet for my competitive nature. I knew nothing about American history prior to my arrival in the United States. Once I was submerged in it, however, I became a politics and history junkie.

Ours was a very hardworking home. Everyone pulled his or her weight. I became the in-house babysitter at age thirteen. Taking care of my little sister Rose became my responsibility, because both my mother and stepfather worked the night shift at the plant and would arrive home at 4:00 a.m.

I know most teenagers struggle with growing pains and issues with their parents. My relationship with my stepfather was no exception. This culminated with a particularly damaging altercation between us. I felt that my stepfather was picking on me by bossing me around. Finally, during one of these aggravating moments, I turned to face him and said, "You're not my father, and you can't tell me what to do." There—I had said it, even though it was incredibly wrong of me to say.

It was certainly the last straw, and my stepfather's anger went out of control. He grabbed me by the shoulders and slammed me against the wall. I did not flinch. I simply croaked, "Go ahead, kill me. I don't care." My mother heard the commotion and came running into the room, trying to pull him away from me. That episode began the long, silent war between us.

While I was growing up, the emphasis in our home was on getting a paying job, not necessarily on academics. With my own children and grandchildren, the mantra I chant is, "Education is your salvation. Seek it everywhere you can."

I was an average student who excelled more in the social graces. I chuckle to myself now, thinking that I once was a straight-A student, except for a B in math in Czechoslovakia. Could it be a language issue? After all, English was my fourth language, after Russian-Carpathian, Slovak, and Russian. Actually, the truth of the matter is, I was having too much fun and leaving too little time for study. I was making up for lost time.

My nemesis back in Slovakia was another girl named Maria. She received all A's and became eligible for the pre-Gimnazia program, which was similar to an honors program—a college preparatory curriculum. I wonder whatever became of Maria's high scholastic achievements. We would have continued to compete fiercely, had I not left for America.

Joan Ignasiak, Chris Messmore (Capt), Jean Seaman, Renee Rolfs, Mary Bobak, Pam Guerne, Andy Til

The Utica High School cheerleading squad

In my sophomore year, a friend, Cathy Turner Seeger, persuaded me to try out for the cheerleading squad. I hesitated at first, not knowing much about the cheers, but then I decided, "Why not?" We cheered our hearts out, but neither of us made the squad. I decided I wasn't going to give up. I practiced the entire year without Cathy, because I couldn't persuade her to try again. I gave it all I had, and the following year, I made the cheerleading squad. "Go Utica Chieftains!"

Me, cheering at football game in my letter sweater

That same year, I entered a talent show sponsored by our local movie theater. To my surprise, I won first place and the prize of twenty-five dollars. I performed my Hungarian Gypsy dance, which my Gypsy friends across the river in Slovakia had taught me. The costume I wore consisted of a black velvet vest with intricate multicolored beading, a white embroidered blouse, and a red skirt. The beautiful, authentic vest was over one hundred years old, and it had been loaned to me by Nanašhka (Godmother). My stepfather's cousin, Mrs. Mary Masyra, and her husband Vasil Masyra were my sister Rose's Godparents. John and Sergie, their two sons, were wonderful to me when I arrived from Europe. Both sons understood and spoke a dialect familiar to me. I can't thank them enough for the help and warmth they showed.

After Nanašhka's death, I wanted to return the beautiful vest to John and his wife, Catherine. Both insisted I keep the vest for the memories it held for me and for my daughters, who would continue the legacy of performing the Hungarian Gypsy dance.

And when my own children were old enough, I assisted Charmaine Schick, owner of Charmaine's Studio of Dance, in choreographing the Gypsy dance for the annual production. I was able to see all three of my daughters perform this dance that was so much a part of my heritage.

Mary Bobak, winner of Utica, Michigan, talent show, performing the Hungarian Gypsy dance

During my junior year of high school, I was chosen by the student body to represent Utica High School at Wolverine Girls' State on the University of Michigan campus in Ann Arbor, Michigan. Girls' State was a nationwide program founded by the American Legion Auxiliary. The original purpose was "to find and develop girls who show inherent leadership tendencies." After 1952, the focus shifted to "inform girls about the duties, privileges, rights and responsibilities of American citizenship and self-government." I had no idea what I was agreeing to experience, but it was an incredible opportunity that will live in my memory forever. This program allowed young women to experience the political process. They were given the opportunity to run for public office, including the Senate, House of Representatives, the judicial branch, and governor. My Nationalist Party encouraged me to seek the governorship position, but I hadn't the foggiest idea where to begin. Most candidates prepared before they even arrived on campus. I didn't have a thought about running for any office. I was there to observe and learn—and have some fun, I must admit.

Someone yelled out, "Mary, you need X number of signatures on the petition to be placed on the ballot." Another girl volunteered to be my campaign manager. Even though I had come for other reasons, I decided to go for it and gratefully accepted her offer of support.

Approximately six hundred girls representing Michigan high schools attended the conference. We were divided into two political parties—Nationalist and Federalist. There was a rigorous campaign, with speeches by candidates promising to do great things for our state of Michigan. After all the hoopla, I became the nominee for governor on the Nationalist ticket. This was my first indoctrination to the political system of electing our leaders. I learned some valuable lessons, which led me to run for public office in the not-so-distant future. I gave my campaign speech—"I Am an American" by Eli Lieberman—in front of both parties. I related to a character in his composition and used it to express my joy and gratefulness.

I imitated him, speaking in a foreign accent, with tears streaming down my face. My heart related to that young girl coming to America just six years ago. The closing sentence was, "I am proud of my new country. I am an Amereekan." The entire student body erupted in cheers, blowing horns, clapping, and whistling. I found it perplexing, and I didn't know how to react. For a change, I actually found myself speechless.

My opponent on the Federalist ticket jumped on the stage beside me and announced she was withdrawing her name from nomination and forwarding her party's votes to me. I was declared governor of Wolverine Girls' State by unanimous vote, the first time in its history. I stood on that stage in a state of shock and thrilled excitement. Pandemonium erupted as I was whisked off the stage and lifted up on the shoulders of young women who were marching around the auditorium halls, declaring me their winner and new governor.

As for me, the excitement was overwhelming and humbling. I couldn't believe how generous and benevolent the American girls were, bestowing this honor upon me. "Why?" I kept asking myself. And all along, my thoughts were that they were more deserving than I was.

The following day I traveled to East Lansing, Michigan, home of Michigan State University, where twelve hundred boys from Michigan high schools were participating in the same political process at Boys' State.

As I stepped onto the stage, Larry Wershky, the governor of Boys' State, presented me with an orchid corsage. The announcer introduced me to the waiting audience. The place erupted with applause, howling, and whistling. After all, these boys hadn't seen a girl in two weeks, or so I was told. Of course, I was in seventh heaven. I knew I wouldn't have another opportunity such as this—me and twelve hundred boys, all to myself! I took my place at the microphone and waved to everyone. A student jumped on top of a chair, shouting, "Hi Mary!"

Straining to see who it was, I immediately recognized my fellow compatriot Wayne Stewart, from Utica High School. "What possessed you to do that?" I asked him later.

He confessed, "The guys didn't believe I knew you, so I had to show them."

Representatives to Boys' State and Girls' State. (L–R)
Wayne Stewart, Charles Beyerlein, Mary Bobak, James Cole

It was a privilege to appear in front of these fine young men and to share my message. In my speech, "What America Means to Me," I shared my gratitude for the many opportunities I had enjoyed since coming to America and my intention to have a positive impact on the future.

As governor of Girls' State, I traveled to area schools, rotary clubs, and Veterans of Foreign Wars groups, expounding on the virtues of this great nation. I always extended my heartfelt thank-you to the veterans for their service and heroism as I related my story of survival during World War II. I would end by expressing my gratitude in this way: "If it were not for you, I would not be here today. Thank you, and God bless you!"

THE **WOLVERINE**
AUXILIAIRE
Volume 5 — Number 1

Miss Mary Bobak, 1956 Governor of Wolverine Girls' State, Utica
Mr. Larry Wershky, 1956 Governor of Wolverine Boys' State, Berkley

AUGUST, 1956

The 1956 magazine cover announcing the two new governors for Wolverine Girls' State and Wolverine Boys' State—Mary Bobak and Larry Wershky

1957 senior prom with my date, Wayne Stewart

Where did senior year go? It flew by so quickly. I enjoyed cheerleading practice, senior play, senior pictures, and planning the senior trip to Washington, DC. Oh, the worrying whether I would be asked to homecoming or the prom! Those trauma-induced years—what fun they were.

Homecoming was a special occasion for me. I was crowned home-coming queen, and my date was a football hero, the infamous guy who stood on top of a chair at the Michigan State auditorium and yelled out, "Hi Mary!"

I was floating on cloud nine when the bandleader called to me, "Hey Queenie! What's your favorite song?" Without hesitation, my answer was "Stardust." It just felt like a "Stardust" type of evening.

The senior trip to our nation's capital was the culmination of our years together as classmates. It was fun, and I can assure you that the teachers had quite a time chaperoning us. Some of our classmates were disappearing artists, who wanted to go exploring on their own. I made arrangements with our district representative for a photo-op on the steps of the Capitol Building. To this day, each visit to Washington, DC, is exciting for me. An essence of great power and wisdom permeates the city. I believe it began with our Founding Fathers creating the phrase,

Homecoming queen, 1956, for Utica High School. (L–R) Vince Angel, Mary Bobak, Ron Seeger. I was surrounded by the co-captains of the football team.

"E Pluribus Unum," meaning out of many, one. This completely resonates with me. The true measure of a country and humankind is to build upon where the previous generations left off. We must learn from the mistakes of the generations before us in order to strengthen and preserve the democratic way of life.

Senior trip to Washington, DC, in 1957

93

Soon, graduation was upon us and senior prom was fast approaching. Who had time to shop for a gown? I finally decided on a replica of the actress Mitzi Gaynor's gown from a movie. It was a strapless, rainbow silk-chiffon number that was as colorful as an aurora borealis. Grandma would've approved!

Looking back at the four years of high school I realize that our class was fairly small. We had one hundred sixty two graduates, and many of them were unique. Our class reunions continue after fifty five years. We meet at a local restaurant for lunch a couple of times a year and spend time catching up on the news and whereabouts of our friends.

After leaving high school, many of our classmates attended local colleges, and some went to college out of state. Others stayed on the farms, continuing their family traditions in agricultural endeavors.

As for me, I was fortunate, because in 1958, I entered and won the Miss Michigan Water Sports title, which awarded me a scholarship to the Patricia Stevens Finishing School, along with a contract for modeling swimwear. I traveled throughout the state, promoting Michigan's water sports and its beautiful waterways. I also participated in aquatic sporting events with a world-champion water skier, which was not an easy task.

The modeling contract enabled me to travel throughout Canada and the Detroit metropolitan area. After my year-long reign was over, I finished my associates degree at Patricia Stevens by attending school at night. By day, I worked at the Chevrolet

Miss Michigan Water Sports queen

Engineering Center in the accounting department. With school and work, I often arrived home after 11:30 p.m. It was a grueling schedule, but I was young and healthy and loved having the opportunities to grow and explore.

I enrolled at Wayne State University in Detroit in August 1958, hoping to finish my coursework for a bachelor's degree. There was only one problem—I didn't have transportation to and from campus. The bus route ended at Eight Mile Road, and I lived at Nineteen Mile Road. I ran into a student from Utica High School and inquired about his schedule. His classes didn't coincide with mine, but I told him I didn't mind waiting until he was done. I would study on campus. We agreed on the price for him to drive me. Classes were scheduled to start in a few weeks.

A few days before the semester was to begin, I received a phone call from him, saying he wouldn't be able to drive me after all..

"Did you drop out?" I asked.

"No, not really," he replied.

"Then why can't you drive me? Do you want more money for gas?"

Hesitating at first, he then blurted out, "Well, my girlfriend doesn't want me to drive you."

I was stunned, dumbfounded actually, and so hurt over this turn of events. As it turned out, I did not attend Wayne State University, because I was unable to find another driver. Instead, I

As a preliminary to Miss America, I entered the Miss Michigan pageant in Muskegon, Michigan, in 1959.

Three of my favorite photos from my modeling career

enrolled at Macomb Community College. I attended classes in the evening and worked as a hostess at Howard Johnson's Restaurant during the day. It was another grueling schedule, carrying sixteen credit hours, participating in the student council, and performing in a stage production portraying a Russian spy named Natasha. I loved it.

That year, I was crowned the first Miss Macomb Community College during the annual Spring Fling dance, as the amazing Stan Kenton Orchestra entertained the crowd.

During the summer break, I auditioned for Matt Gouzey's dance troupe. The group was composed of college students attending various colleges and universities in the Midwest. Several students in the troupe had immigrated from Eastern Europe, Central Europe, Italy, and Greece. I auditioned with the fiery Gypsy dance. One judge remarked, "She's a diamond in the rough. Give her a couple of weeks of intensive training, and she'll do great."

Boy, when they say intensive training, they mean intensive. With bleeding blisters, taped ankles, and calluses on the bottoms of my feet, I was in excruciating pain. I doubted if I could last for two weeks. The ballet bar work, with continuous stretching, allowed me to show some signs of progress. Once we conquered the basics, we began learning the dance routines. Folk dances from around the world were balletic in nature. The boys played a variety of instruments—accordion, balalaika, violin, guitar, and clarinet. They sang songs in their native languages, while the girls performed the dances. Occasionally, the boys would join in a dance if a partner was required. "Matt Gouzey's Temberitzans" was the logo on the bus that transported us to various destinations. We performed in Chicago, Canada, and Detroit and appeared on television, in clubs, and at various ethnic organizations. At the end of summer, we began to disperse for our respective colleges. Our tuition was paid partially by Matt Gouzey, as payment for our performances. The group would reunite the following summer and continue performing.

Before I left, I let Mr. Gouzey and his daughter, Terrie (our truant officer), know how much I enjoyed the experience. I told them, however, that I would not be returning next year. I needed a rest. They understood. They told me I would be missed, especially my chocolate chip cookies! A hungry troupe, it was.

After a year of travel as Miss Michigan Water Sports, along with runway shows, photo shoots, and appearances on television and radio, I was feeling like a nomad living out of a suitcase. I needed roots, a home, and to finish my education. My dream was to work in an embassy, preferably in Eastern Europe, utilizing my language skills.

I continued my education and sporadic modeling jobs and, of course, all along I was looking for Prince Charming. Isn't there a saying in the English lexicon, "The way to a man's heart is through his stomach"? My hostess job at Howard Johnson's paid off. The guy was hungry, and I filled his stomach. After fifty-three years, I am still filling it.

This drawing was done by my
granddaughter Abigail Boutrous. Her title:
"Grandpa Bob and Grandma Mary"

Chapter Twenty-Three
THERE'S SOMETHING ABOUT BOB

It's funny how dreams change as we age. I can recall my dreams as a child—so simple, hoping for one chocolate bar after the next. When I grew older, I dreamed of my Prince Charming sweeping me off of my feet. Well, it didn't happen quite that way. Bob and I met when he and a friend, Don Kingsley, were attending a golf outing at a nearby golf club. They stopped at the Howard Johnson's Restaurant where I was employed as a hostess for the summer. Don was friendly and animated, while Bob was rather grumpy and didn't want to chitchat early in the morning. Both men returned to the restaurant a few days later, dressed in blazers, shirts, and ties, as though they were attending a party or a theater performance. Bob's demeanor had changed since his last visit; he was friendlier, smiled more, and stopped me as I passed by for more coffee and water. Both asked my name and how long had I worked at Howard Johnson's. I told them I was a student, and this was my summer employment. By the time they left the restaurant, my shift was almost over.

As I was about to go home, the evening hostess told me I had a phone call. It was Bob, who introduced himself and reminded me who he was by saying that he and his friend had just left the restaurant. "Well, which one are you?" I asked. "The short one, or the tall one?"

There was a pause and then he blurted out, "The short one." "Oh!" I quipped. (I don't think he has ever forgiven me for that one.) He continued, "Well, can I have your phone number?"

My immediate answer was, "Of course not!"

"Pardon me?" he shot back.

"I can't give you my phone number because I don't know you!" I exclaimed.

He was persistent. "How am I supposed to get to know you if you won't even give me your phone number?" he asked.

I thought for a second and then responded, "Well, I guess you're right. I suppose I can give you the number, since our phone is unlisted."

He laughed. "I know. I already tried to find it!"

His persistence kindled my curiosity, so I gave him my phone number.

He phoned later, and we arranged a dinner date for the following week, after my last class ended. Actually, I had to cut a class; otherwise, it would've been too late for dinner. I had taken great care in dressing that evening—sleek black dress, triple strand of pearls, and black high heels, not my usual attire for classes. As I came out of the building and stepped onto the terrace, I saw fellow classmates congregating, smoking their Lucky Strikes and Camel cigarettes. (This was the late '50s.) They teased me relentlessly, asking me where I was going all dolled up. Spotting Bob walking toward the entrance, I made a quick exit away from the peering eyes and whistling cat calls of my classmates.

Bob whisked me away, chuckling to himself about all the commotion.

"They're just a bunch of guys, clowning around," I said. He led me down the street to what I presumed was his car, and I waited for him to open the door. He informed me that I was waiting in front of the wrong car. He walked me to a white Cadillac Coupe de Ville. I had been well trained at Patricia Stevens Finishing School about how to gracefully get in and out of a car. But this time, while smiling at my escort, I fell into the car with hands and legs flailing. I just wasn't expecting my date to be driving a car that resembled a limo. As I collected my wits, I asked, "Is this your car?"

"Actually, no, I borrowed it. My new car is on order. It should arrive in a couple of weeks," he responded.

Yeah, I thought, he's trying to impress me.

As we drove past the crowd gathered on the steps, I saw their bulging eyeballs and wagging tongues. My response to them was very theatrical. Coquettishly, I raised my nose up in the air as we drove by the gawkers.

Bob and I shared an informative dinner, as he asked me a million questions. All I found out about him was that he had graduated from Michigan State University and was working in a lumberyard. He had a younger sister and an older brother. I told him I wanted to work in the diplomatic field and become an interpreter, preferably in one of the Eastern European countries. It ended up being a very pleasant evening. After dinner, he drove me back to my car—actually my parents' Olds 88—still parked in the campus lot. He walked me to my car and asked if he could call me again. I thanked him for a lovely evening and said YES.

He called again, and this time he picked me up at my home. Before he was due to arrive, I rushed out to the dry cleaners to pick up my raincoat. He arrived early. Dad was on his lawnmower, cutting the grass, when Bob arrived and asked if I was home. Dad told him he was the gardener and didn't know. I arrived in time to apologize for my dad and

Bob and Mary at the Michigan vs. Michigan State football game

for not being there when he arrived. He laughed, remarking that Dad was a character.

The city of Ann Arbor was our destination because Bob's alma mater was playing the University of Michigan. I was presented with a white Fuji mum with a green S for Michigan State. After the victorious football game, we attended a party at the Kappa Sigma fraternity house, where I met many of Bob's fraternity brothers and friends. The weather couldn't have been more cooperative; it was a magnificent, sunny fall day and the beginning of a beautiful courtship.

When I got home, Mother stuck her head in the bedroom and inquired about my date. "I think this is the guy," I replied. Of course, she just rolled her eyes—I must have used that line before.

Bob and I dated for a year and were married on September 17, 1960, at the First Presbyterian Church of Mt. Clemens. The reception took place at the golf club where Bob and his friend Don went to golf that fateful morning when we first met. The "tall" one was a groomsman at our wedding, along with Bob's brother, Dennis. My sister, Rose Ann, was my maid of honor, and Bob's sister, Grace, was a bridesmaid. Cousin Ann's four-year-old daughter, Sheral Wilson, was the darling flower girl. We honeymooned in Ft. Lauderdale, Florida—along with a torrential downpour for five solid days. We walked around without shoes in ankle-deep water. The sun finally appeared, allowing me to swim in the ocean for the first time. It was old hat for Bob; his parents had owned efficiency apartments in Ft. Lauderdale for many years. He was used to frolicking in the surf. When we returned to our home in Roseville,

Our engagement announcement in the local newspaper

102

Our wedding day, September 17, 1960

Michigan, we discovered that the bedroom furniture hadn't arrived. We spent the next two weeks sleeping on the floor.

Bob continued working in the family business, Groesbeck Lumber Company, and I continued my schooling. Our home was constantly being worked on. Bob was changing, adding, removing, building, and remodeling. Two years later, we had our first daughter, Leslie, a bundle of joy who cried for hours on end with colic. The sleepless nights seemed endless. As with all parents, we placed so much attention on the firstborn; it must have been suffocating for the child. We watched every move, every breath, to see if she was still breathing. The menu was carefully balanced to ensure that Leslie was getting the proper nutrition. It was a far cry from the nutrition I was fed—and I survived. Leslie was an independent handful.

Two and a half years later, our second daughter, Jennifer, was born. She was a quiet, content child. She slept throughout the night, probably sensing that I couldn't survive another colicky child. The two girls played and fought together, as most siblings do. In the meantime, Bob kept building, adding a playhouse, tennis court, and a swimming pool. In the winter, he flooded the tennis court and turned it into an ice rink. Six years later, our third daughter, Nicole, came along. She was a blonde, blue-eyed little doll for her sisters to play with. They would take her up and down the neighborhood in her buggy and show her off to all of their friends. They were very excited for about two weeks, and then the excitement wore off. "Here, Mom, you can have her," they said. They had more important things to do.

It was a wonderful neighborhood with plenty of young families with children of all ages. We looked out for one another, always keeping a close watch over the children.

Our three daughters grew up to become attorneys; we call this "girl power" around our house. We're thinking about hanging a wooden shingle with the inscription, "Sisters in Law." Bob decided to adopt a male cat named Oscar to keep us girls in line.

It's difficult to give yourself a pat on the back, but I wonder if all parents shouldn't do this once in a while—pat each other on the back and say, "We tried to do a good job, and it looks like we may have succeeded."

Sisters in Law

Family photo on our 50th wedding anniversary

Chapter Twenty-Four
RETURN TO GRANDFATHER

Unfortunately, I had no contact with my father after I left for America in 1949. Twenty years later, I went back to visit my former home with my two daughters. Leslie was then six years old, and Jennifer was four. My mother and my cousin Maryanne also joined us, but we were on different flights. We connected with them in Vienna, Austria. I rented a car for our trip, and we started off together for the drive to Czechoslovakia in July 1969.

We were stopped at the checkpoint near Slovakia. The guards with uniforms and guns came to the car and asked for passports, car registration, and my international driver's license. I got out of the car to hand over my passport. The remaining passports were passed to them as well. I started speaking to them in Russian, telling them that the car registration was in my suitcase, which was stored in the trunk. I tried opening the trunk, but it wouldn't budge. I kept wiggling the key every which way in an attempt to open that darn trunk. The guards were becoming impatient, informing me that crossing the border was not possible without registration papers. I gave them my car keys to see if they could open the trunk with their strength. To their surprise, they couldn't figure out how to open it either.

The sight of guards with guns questioning me frightened the children. I was also frightened and upset but tried to put on a brave face in front of my daughters. I told the guards that I was keeping a promise, which involved coming back to see my grandfather. His only wish was to see me once more before he passed away. They led me into a building to consult the commissioner. I followed them into the office, shaking with fear, while looking back at the car where the children, my mother, and cousin Maryanne were sitting. I stood before the commissioner, who looked like a bloated bullfrog sitting behind his desk. One of the guards handed our passports to this menacing man. He scrutinized them and then began interrogating me. "How can it be that everyone was born in the United States except you?" he asked.

I had to go through the entire story again—how my grandparents had immigrated to the USA, got married, had seven children, and then returned to Czechoslovakia. Mother married my father, a Czechoslovakian citizen. I was born in 1939, before my mother departed for America. She had been told that she would lose her American citizenship if she did not return before she reached the age of twenty-one. She planned to send for me, but then my father was drafted into the Czechoslovakia army, leaving me in the care of my maternal grandparents. We survived the war, and I traveled to America in 1949 to live with my mother. Thus, I was able to hold a dual citizenship.

He kept studying me like a test subject as I rambled on. By this time, I was becoming very nervous. The commissioner cleared his throat and asked to view the car registration papers. I didn't know what to do, since they were packed into the stuck trunk. I gingerly placed the key on his desk, and nearly sobbing, I croaked, "Here you go. Open it!"

He glared at me with disdain, offended by my ordering him to do such a menial task. The guards were sympathetic toward me, as they were young, and I was only twenty-nine at the time. Miniskirts were in fashion, which is exactly what I was wearing. I was decked out in a mini dress, high heels, and had my hair styled in a bouffant bubble cut, AKA the Jackie Kennedy look. All of a sudden, the guards surrounded the bullfrog commissioner. A flurry of whispering took place behind the human wall. When they exited the huddle they informed me that we were allowed to cross the border into Slovakia. I was elated, and

*Leslie, Jennifer, and me (with the Jackie Kennedy look),
before our trip to Czechoslovakia*

extended my hand to the frog. He uttered a few words before I handed him a pack of cigarettes and chewing gum. He then sneered at me, but I didn't care, as my dilemma had ended happily. I came out of the building, followed by a contingency of guards, and I began handing the young men packs of gum and cigarettes. I knew those were the hot items behind the Iron Curtain.

I was free to cross the border, but I wondered if I could freely travel back across when our visits were over. I questioned one of the guards, and he assured me I wouldn't have a problem. I wasn't so sure, so I kept mentioning the frog commissioner. Their reply about him was, "Oh, he's just an old goat trying to adhere to every little rule."

In spite of their reassurance, I continued to feel uneasy. When I finally got back to the car, the girls were crying with fear. Mother was terrified, and Maryanne was in a state of shock. "We can go!" I exclaimed. I put the keys in the ignition, started the car, and crossed the border. We were off on our journey.

I quickly assured everyone that everything was fine, and we would not have any problems coming back. Sighs of relief were audible as I relayed the good news. Not knowing where to stop for lodging, we drove into the night. I cautiously followed a bus, the only visible lights on the mountainous horizon. The bus stopped, and I asked the young man who exited if there was a hotel nearby.

He was giving me directions when he noticed the tired and confused expression on my face. "Never mind," he said. "I'll go with you to point out the way to lodging." He informed us that he was a soccer player coming back from a game. We were grateful for the man's kindness. He really did go out of his way to help us. I attempted to pay him for his trouble, but he wouldn't hear of it. We thanked him again as he pointed at the hotel in the distance. When we arrived, we piled into the hotel with a can of Lysol. The girls spotted ants in the bathtub, so I was inclined to spray every inch of the room with it. After my task of exterminating bugs was over, I tried to settle the girls down, but they wouldn't go to sleep. So I made adjustments. Our makeshift sleeping arrangement involved leaving the bathroom light on and sleeping in our clothes.

Awakened by the first rays of sunlight, we splashed water on our faces and headed for my aunt's home. When our crew arrived at Aunt Justina's in Zalužiçe, the welcome was warm and tearful. My aunt's husband, Andrej Tahla, was now a police administrator in a local town, but he was home for our arrival. He tried unsuccessfully to remove our suitcases from the trunk of the car. I began toying with the button next to the lock, simultaneously pressing it along with inserting the key, and the trunk popped open! It was a Mercedes-Benz that I had never driven, so I was unfamiliar with the locking mechanism. I selected it because it was the only car for rent with an automatic transmission.

Happy to have access to our belongings once again, we unpacked and were ready to begin our visit. But first, Uncle Andrej had to take me to the local police station so I could register, to acknowledge that my family was in the country. I needed to register in each town that we stayed in. Uncle Andrej led me into the chief of police's office. I shook his hand and then sat down for a chat. I handed him our passports.

He proceeded to mark our names on a pad of paper and said that he hoped I would enjoy my visit. I assured him that I was excited to see my family. I inquired if he smoked, and when he said yes, I handed him a pack of cigarettes and some gum. He opened the pack and slipped a cigarette into his mouth.

The chief asked me about my trip to Czechoslovakia and how I liked it so far. I explained that I was here because of a promise to my grandfather that I would come back to visit him. I went on to tell the head of police that Grandpa had raised me until I made the voyage to America at age ten. He listened, fascinated, as I unfolded the war stories that were so real and memorable to my family. I talked about leaving for America by myself, not knowing what my own mother's face looked like. I could see the police chief was enjoying the cigarette, inhaling deeply and exhaling slowly. We both felt relaxed in each other's company.

He pointedly asked, "Would you like to live here again?"

I looked at him in disbelief. "Are you kidding? No, I would not want to come back to live here."

I thought my uncle was going to have a stroke after hearing what I said. He slid further down in his chair, probably from embarrassment. The chief didn't miss a beat, asking, "Well, why not?"

I replied, "I have a lot more freedom and opportunities in the United States than you have here. I can travel anywhere I want in the world, but you can't travel to the United States."

He stopped me. "Yes, we can travel to the USA," he interjected, "but we can't afford the price you Americans charge for a plane ticket."

"Why don't you fly your own planes to the United States and use your own currency for pricing?" I egged him on, informing him that he would be welcomed with open arms into America for a visit.

He laughed and joked further about the differences between America and Czechoslovakia. I could see that he wanted to continue our playful debate, but my uncle was dying a slow death, not knowing what this would lead him into. At that point, Uncle Andreĵ thanked the chief and inquired if there was any more paperwork for me to complete. The chief replied, "No, everything is in order." He told me I could stop in any time if I had any questions or concerns or just to visit. I flashed back a Cheshire cat smile, thanked him for a most enjoyable debate, and shook his hand before leaving with my uncle. Uncle Andreĵ walked behind me, wiping the sweat from his brow.

We visited with Auntie Justina and Uncle Andreĵ for a few more days and got reacquainted, and I realized that I needed to hone my language skills. I had to ask everyone to speak slowly as my brain became acclimated to translating. My head hurt from the task.

Once we left Zalužiĉe and headed for Ćertizne, my quest to see Grandfather began. The anticipation was tremendous. I wondered what his reaction might be, as he didn't know that we were coming. My mother wanted to surprise him. I worried that perhaps he couldn't handle the

Entrance to the village of Ćertizne in 1969

excitement, but Mother wouldn't budge on her idea of a surprise visit. As we neared the village, my worries about our arrival escalated. We drove along a bumpy dirt road. I was taking in the sights when I noticed the flowered cross on the right side of the road. These crosses could be found at the entrances to small villages throughout the countryside. It was common to place flowers around the crosses. I stopped the car, made the sign of the cross, and smiled at the sweet memories of my childhood. I felt ready to proceed up the hill to the village. Everything appeared smaller than I remembered it to be. The road seemed narrower, the homes smaller, the hills not as high. One thing was different: there were electrical lines standing tall in the village of my lost childhood. Finally, something had replaced the kerosene lamps we had used for lighting.

As we passed the first four homes, we came upon the place I remembered. There was a gated fence with an older man standing there, possibly waiting to see if he would receive any mail. I stopped the car as he looked up, a puzzled look on his face. "There he is! Don't startle him!" I told my mother. She jumped out of the car, shouting, "Ňaňu, Ňaňu!" (Daddy, Daddy!) The poor man was dazed as Mother hugged and kissed him. He was crying and was visibly shaken. I slowly got out of the car and walked over to him, giving him a kiss and a hug. "Grandpa, I kept my promise," I said. Tears streamed down his face, mingling with mine.

My poor children stood awkwardly by the car with cousin Maryanne. They were frightened and didn't know what was going on, so they began to cry as well. I assured them that everything was fine because the tears were tears of joy. Once my grandfather calmed down, we walked to his house to greet the remaining family. There was much excitement, delight, and recollections of times past. Aunt Ĵevka and her husband (whom I didn't have fond memories of) were happy to see me. Their daughter, Haňňa, had married Ivan. They too resided in Grandfather's home now. Haňňa had been about two years old when I left for America.

We visited with relatives and neighbors and strolled about the village, starting conversations with the people we met. I stopped by my teacher's home across the river. She was rinsing something in the water when I approached her. I greeted her in the native language, saying, "Dobry deň Uchitelka Ostapçhikanya." (Good day, Teacher Ostapçhikanya.) She eyed me curiously, and then a smile appeared on her lips while her eyes lit up with happiness. She extended her arms and said, "Maria Hochova?"

"How did you know it was me?" I asked.

"Your eyes, those expres-

My beloved grandfather, Andreĵ Śafran

sive eyes, and your infectious laugh!" she replied. I reminded her that she had made quite an impression on a countless number of young students. She had been a wonderful teacher and always encouraged us to keep on learning. I introduced her to my daughters and gave her a gift from America—chewing gum and cigarettes!

I also passed around dollar bills; US currency was worth a lot more than the Slovak korunas. They probably sold the dollars on the black market, a service that offered better exchange rates than the bank. Other villagers approached me and asked if I could sell them the American money. I certainly didn't want to get into any legal trouble in Czechoslovakia, so I politely refused their requests. It's one thing to give money to relatives as a gift, but to exchange it over the black market is a different matter entirely.

On our second night at Grandpa's, we were all quite exhausted from the excitement. Traveling was an emotional roller coaster, and we eagerly anticipated a good night's sleep.

We had just drifted to a peaceful sleep when a loud banging on the back door echoed throughout the house. I heard a man's voice wailing, "Marya, Marya, moĵa zlata ribka." (My little Mary, my goldfish.) Everyone was awakened from sleep. Grandpa assured us he would take care of Nikolaĵ. It was, of course, my father, wanting to see me. I was ready to go speak with him when Grandpa insisted that he would handle this matter. He was crippled with a fear that my father would harm my mother out of anger because she had left for America so long ago. In his anger, he once had threatened to kill her if he ever laid eyes on her again. All of us were fearful, especially my mother. Grandpa left the house and locked the door behind him. I assured my girls that everything was okay, and I coaxed them back to sleep. I falsely informed them that someone was out late, celebrating, and that Grandpa was simply taking care of the noisy problem.

The next morning, I was even more exhausted but I decided that I would drive alone to Habura to see my father and settle things. Everyone was extremely anxious after the previous night's experience. For me, though, it was a bit hard to understand their fright because the man was my father, after all, my flesh and blood. After driving to what I thought was his home, I got out of the car cautiously. I approached a man picking peapods in the garden. He wore a faded blue beret on his head and an old worn-out uniform of some kind. I stopped at the fence to ask if he was Nikolaĵ Hoç. He dropped his hoe, came to the fence, and confirmed my suspicion. I was taken aback by his appearance, as I remembered his handsome looks from twenty years before when he was in his early thirties.

My mother had often told me about what a drunk, womanizing abuser he could be. It's a puzzle as to what degree you really know a person after a short amount of time spent together. He was drafted into the Czechoslovakian army during their first year of marriage, and was later wounded by a shrapnel blast to his left shoulder.

Softly, I said, "Ňaňu, ja vašha divka Marya." (Dad, I am your daughter Mary.) He stood there, staring in disbelief. Finally, he extended his hand to shake mine. I was dumbfounded—I'd expected a hug, a kiss, or even a warmer reception. He removed his beret and scratched his very sparsely haired head. What a sad reunion, I thought. The last time I saw him, he had a very dark, thick, and wavy head of hair. He was barely recognizable. And he greeted me like a stranger, which, in truth, I guess I was. I told him that I had fulfilled my promise of visiting from America. He stood there and looked at me and neither of us knew what to say or do next. Being tired and worn, I decided to just say good-bye and drive away.

The following morning at the break of dawn, I slipped out of the house while everyone was still sound asleep. I groggily trudged to the highest point in the backyard, where I sat down under the cherry tree. There, I began to let go of everything I had kept inside of me all those years. I cried and cried until I had no tears left. I was twenty-nine years old and the tears had been saved up from a lifetime of always being strong and resilient. I finally wiped my face just as the sun began to filter through the cherry tree's branches.

I picked some cherries to eat, and then I attempted to see how far I could spit the cherry pits. It felt good to play such a childish and innocent game…just as I used to play it as a kid. I looked around the hills that fascinated me in the morning light, and I began to reminisce about my childhood days. I recalled how we used to slide down the hill on the bits and pieces of cardboard left behind from the war. In the fall, the grasses on the hill turned silver and became very slippery. We would drag pieces of cardboard up the hill, sit as many of us as could fit on the scrap pieces, and come zooming down the slope while screaming to our hearts' content. Many times, we would fall off when we hit the bottom of the hill.

Winter was always fun, with the wooden sleds everyone in the village made for their household. Spring was mushroom-picking time in the woods, accompanied by the elders who explained which mushrooms were safe to eat. In the summertime, there was much work to be done. We planted wheat, potatoes, and vegetables and cultivated these crops.

We picked strawberries deep in the forest, along with blueberries, rosehips for tea, and hazelnuts.

My cousins, twins Michael and Marya, lived next door. They were a few years older and more or less in charge of the young ones while we gathered the fruits, nuts, and fungi in the forest. I recall one occasion when we were frolicking and skipping while gathering blueberries from the bushes. We were placing them into our pails when we encountered three black snakes. Somebody screamed, "Snakes! Run!" We scrambled to grab our pails and sprinted away from the scary, slithering creatures. They coiled in a circle and sprang out after us. We ran faster while spreading out in different directions to confuse them. We were pretty much gasping with exhaustion by the time we finally escaped from that blueberry patch of peril!

On scalding summer days, we would go down to the river and splash, jump, and play in the water and skip stones across the water to see who could make more waves. The west side of the river was where the gypsies came every summer, looking for work. They set up camp in the clearing. They traveled by wagon and built huts to reside in on those hot days. We watched them from a distance, and we were told not to mingle with them because they were known to steal children. Naturally, we were curious and eyed them suspiciously. We used to hear them singing and dancing around the bonfire at night. They were great musicians and played at the village weddings. I decided that I wanted to see the dancing at a closer range and really hear the violins, accordions, and tambourines that were so beautifully laced with ribbons. The gypsies were dressed in long, colorful skirts and embroidered blouses, and they had long black braids hanging down their backs.

They discovered me watching them one day and called for me to join them in their festivities. As I skipped over to join them, the men started playing a haunting melody on their violins, a song I didn't recognize. I loved the sound of that music. As the gypsies played on, the women grabbed their tambourines and began dancing in a circular pattern. I was mesmerized by this display, and when I was handed a tambourine, I took it and began to shake and then strike it in the center, just like the women. They laughed joyously and instructed me to the rhythm of the melody. I kept practicing until they nodded that I was getting it. After that came the steps to the dance. I watched carefully, in sheer determination that I would perfect the steps along with the tambourine. I had a great summer learning the routines and dancing with the gypsies.

When I won the talent show in the United States when I was fourteen, I'd performed a Hungarian Gypsy dance with my tambourine to the music of the Hungarian Symphony No. 2. That music still haunts me to this day.

During the wee hours of that morning in Czechoslovakia, I thought about my friends from those long-ago days. I was disappointed that I couldn't visit them on this trip; I had so many questions to ask. Most of them had moved away from the village into bigger cities, looking for a better way of life. If I'd had more time, I would have tried to locate and visit them.

Then the sun came up, warming me and drying the dew on the grass and trees. I had written some notes while sitting under the cherry tree. I had tried to describe my feelings about returning twenty years later to my homeland. I became teary-eyed again and decided to go back to the house before anyone realized I was missing.

There is never enough time to see everyone you want to visit or to explore the places that have haunted your memory. Grandfather, Mother, Maryanne, Uncle Andrej, and I made a trip to Dukla. Grandpa wanted us to see a memorial monument that was erected after World War II to commemorate citizens who participated in the war effort to feed soldiers. Grandma would bake loaves of bread and take them to the camp to feed our troops. An old photograph was on display at the memorial, and Grandma was one of the people in it. Grandpa was so proud of the picture and the monument that he wanted us to see it. It was a touching moment for me. I snapped a picture of the monument, and I was grateful to Grandpa for the experience.

While the adults in our group traveled to the historical site, my daughters, Leslie and Jennifer, were left in the care of Aunt Justina, and cousins Mañja, Ĺuba, and Michael. They played with the chickens, chasing them around the yard for fun. What good sports they were, as they communicated by gestures, pictures, and sound because nobody there spoke English. I still marvel at my beautiful little girls and how they adapted to the strange surroundings and coped with the language barrier.

At one point during our visit, my mother and I drove by my father's village. The car got stuck in the gravel between the river and my father's house. I kept spinning my wheels, spewing gravel in all directions. Father must have heard all the commotion, because he came out of his house. He called to some men down the road, and they rushed over to help. They pushed back and forth, finally moving the car enough to release it from the hole I created. Father then spotted my mother in the backseat and inquired who she was. "She's my mother," I said.

"Tell her to come to the house," he replied. He headed up the hill to his home as I tried to convince Mother to follow me. She kept refusing until Father's wife walked down to our car and asked her to join them. Reluctantly, Mother climbed out of the car and trailed us into their home.

Let me explain the dynamics. After my mother left for America and settled in the Detroit area, she met Julian Bobak and divorced my father. Father was extremely angry and upset. As I've mentioned, he vowed that if he ever laid eyes on her again, he would kill her. Although that was almost thirty years ago, the thought of it made my mother and me quite nervous to be there with him. We were jumpy and uncomfortable. My father asked Mother why she hadn't wanted to come into his home. Mother simply shrugged her shoulders. I tried to fill the gaps in the conversation with nervous chatter. Father made a remark about her blonde hair, because he remembered her as a brunette. She shrugged again, making the situation even more awkward. I was about ready to jump out of my skin when he got up and left the room. I thought of placing myself in front of my mother in case he came back with a gun, but he returned holding a bottle of alcohol and four glasses. He carefully poured himself a glass of whatever it was, but the rest of us declined the drinks, although I could've used one at that moment.

After a few gulps of the golden liquid, he began to relax and started asking questions about my life and cracking a joke here or there. In between responses, I began to see the similarities in our personalities. He had a good sense of humor and was gregarious and sociable. My mother, however, was quite the opposite. She was serious, stoic at times, and insecure. I recognized the dynamic between the occupants of the room. Father's new wife was a sturdy woman—tall, square, and with no shape to her. I can't remember her hair color because she wore a scarf tied to her head, but she had a ruddy, freckled complexion. She was very gracious to my mother and me. I wondered if she noticed the obvious difference in appearance between Mother and her. Mother was dressed to the teeth in modern western attire with a beautiful head of blonde hair.

I reflected and realized that my gene pool resembled my Father's. I had always complained about my hair—or the lack thereof. As a child, I always considered my short, fine, flyaway ringlets a curse. I joke about it now, saying that I have three hairs on my head to braid, but my hairdressers, Augustino Giordano and Lou Macia, do a wonderful job of managing my unruly hair. They are not only beauticians but a couple of magicians.

Father and his new wife had two daughters. The younger one resembled her mother, while the older one looked like a carbon copy of me. She was named Maria, which unnerved me. Who in the world gives his kid the same name as a child from a previous marriage? I wonder what their daughter thought when meeting me for the first time. A few days later, my half-sisters, cousin Vera, and I were driving to visit some relatives, when out of the blue, the other Maria asked me a question. "What kind of daughter are you, not writing to your father all these years?"

I swerved the car, put it in park, and turned to her. Pointing my finger at her, I exclaimed, "Where was my father for ten years while my grandmother and grandfather raised me? They were my parents for the first ten years of my life!" She didn't say a word in reply. I turned back, shifted the car into drive and pulled out of there with gravel flying behind me. How dare she attack me without knowing the facts. There were so many raw emotions coursing through me during this return visit to my birthplace. It was difficult at times, yet I knew I would always be grateful for coming and for giving my own children the opportunity to see where I was born and to meet my beloved grandfather, their great-grandfather.

At last, though, it was time for the journey to come to an end. It was not easy for me to leave the village of my childhood. I knew this was my final visit with Grandfather. Mother and Maryanne were staying for another couple of weeks. As I said farewell to my extended family, I promised to keep in touch via mail. My already frail heart was breaking from saying good-bye to Grandfather. But I was able to leave with a smile, because I knew he was proud of the woman I had become, and he was happy that I had kept my promise to visit him.

Driving the winding road away from the village, I felt strongly that I was blessed to be returning to America, my wonderful new homeland. My intent was to say good-bye to my father, so I made one last stop to give my father and his family gifts of money, cigarettes, and gum. To my amazement, he asked me if I could send him a motorized saw for cutting down trees. I said, "Sure, Dad, I'll send you one." I didn't know at the time how heavy it was. When I told my husband about the saw, he agreed, but it ended up costing over five hundred dollars for the saw and the shipping to Czechoslovakia. As soon as the package arrived, I received a letter, written by the other Maria, stating that Father thanked me for the saw. She then proceeded to list around fifteen other items she wanted me to send to her. I didn't send any of the products she requested. And I never heard from her or my father again.

Chapter Twenty-Five
My Father's Family

As I've shared throughout my story, I spent very little time with my father. I did, however, spend time with his family, and I want to tell a little of their story too. After all, they are all part of my family tree.

My father's parents lived in the village of Habura. They had three sons and two daughters. The sons were Michael (Mike), the youngest; Pavel (Paul), the middle son; and my father, Nikolaĵ, the oldest. While my father had the dark Latin appearance, Uncle Paul was fair-skinned with light hair and blue eyes. Uncle Mike was a combination of both. I learned that Uncle Michael died in his mother's arms, at age fifteen, after being struck by the butt of a Gestapo rifle. He was down in the cellar of Grandma and Grandpa Hoç's home when the Gestapo stormed into the cellar. They interrogated him and wrongly accused him of being a partisan. Both he and Grandma Kristina pleaded with the Nazi police, claiming that Michael was just a young boy and would never be a partisan. But the angry and suspicious Gestapo struck Uncle Mike on his right temple as he struggled to stand. After the harsh blow to his head, he fell into his mother's arms and died. While Grandma was holding her dead son's body, the Gestapo heartlessly stomped out of the cellar, warning everyone that they would be punished if they were found to be associated with the partisans.

I interacted with Grandma Hoç more than the other family members. I found her to be a warm, social, fun-loving grandmother. Grandpa Hoç stayed to himself. He was unusually quiet and loved working in the barn, tending to the animals. Grandma, on the other hand, was the mover and the shaker, so to speak. She was the social one. I once witnessed her retrieving a silver flask from under her long skirt and sipping some liquid refreshment. She was a happy, friendly soul. (Hm-m-m…I wonder what was in that flask.)

One morning, I decided that I wanted to visit Grandma Hoç in Habura. I persuaded my friend Anna to go with me, promising her lots of candy from Grandma's general store. Anna was reluctant at first, but the lure of all those sweets finally made her agree to join me. The distance to Habura was longer than I had anticipated, and Anna kept whining and asking how much farther we needed to go. And all the while I was thinking of the Big Bad Wolf getting us before we ever made it to Grandmother's.

We finally showed up at her doorstep. "How did you get here, Marya?" she asked.

"Oh, we walked here by ourselves," I replied.

Grandma's eyes widened as she said, "How are you going to get back? It will soon be dark."

"That's all right, Grandma. We will walk fast," I chirped. She told us to step inside, and she offered us some water. "You must be thirsty by now," she said.

We both nodded our heads. "Yes!" I said, "it's warm outside and that was a long walk!"

She then led us to the front of the house, where a small country store was attached. She instructed us to pick out some candies and put them in a bag for the return journey. Of course, my friend Anna and I were delighted. Aunt Mary looked at me with a jaundiced eye. Most likely she was thinking, "Here's that pesky kid again, dipping into my profits!" Anna and I picked out our favorite candies, dropped them in a bag, thanked Grandma Hoç, and ignored Aunt Mary's glaring eyes.

We were ready to leave when Grandma spotted a neighbor going to Çertizne and asked him if he would mind dropping us off at our home. He readily agreed and told us to jump in his cart. He signaled the horse with the pull of the reins and off we rode, waving good-bye to Grandma.

As we got closer to home, trepidation began to set in. We knew what the consequences would be and that angry people would be waiting for us. There was Grandfather, with the exasperated look on his face, pulling his hair, saying, "What am I to do with you?"

"Grandpa, I brought back some chocolate for you from Baba Hoć," I said as I handed him the chocolate. I sensed I was about to be court-martialed, and I wanted to cushion the blow with sweets. My friend Anna was forbidden to play with me ever again. But we figured that after the storm blew over, we could be best friends again.

My father's brother Uncle Paul was the person I remember the most fondly. My earliest recollection of Uncle Paul was at a relative's home. Uncle Paul and I sat outdoors at a picnic table. We were playing Find the Walnut. It involved three cups and a walnut. He would place a walnut under the first cup and then begin to move all three cups slowly back and forth. Then he would stop and ask me to guess which cup held the walnut. I always thought I was following the path of the walnut, but every time I was wrong. I was becoming frustrated and agitated, so Uncle Paul began to move the cups ever so slowly. I kept my eye on the table, and this time I found the walnut. I squealed with delight and thought that Uncle Paul was just the nicest uncle in the whole wide world. My prize was that I got to crack the walnut with a stone, and I savored the delicious crunchy texture and nutty taste.

Sometime after that meeting, Uncle Paul was shipped to Russia to fight the oncoming sea of German soldiers. He worked as a cook in the army. He was killed by the partisans in Russia and left behind a loving wife.

One of my father's sisters, Aunt Mary, lived with Grandma and Grandpa Hoć along with her husband, Seman, and son Andrej. The younger sister, Haňňa, died while giving birth to a child named Verka. Verka later immigrated to America, searching for something more than she was able to find in Czechoslovakia. Grandmother Hoć died soon after the war. I wonder if it wasn't from a broken heart after losing two sons and a daughter. Grandpa Hoç lived to an old age and resided with his daughter Mary and her family.

Many years after my visit to Czechoslovakia with my daughters, my father passed away. Unfortunately, I didn't learn of his death until six months after it happened. My aunt had written to my mother, informing her of his death, but Mother didn't tell me. Once I became aware of his passing, I wrote to Aunt Jevka, wanting to know if my father had a proper headstone on his grave. I wanted to send money to purchase one if he did not have one. Aunt Jevka wrote back and assured me that he had a beautiful headstone, and I felt at peace.

Although much of what I know of my father's family has been passed down to me in stories over the years, I still feel connected to them, and I wanted them to be a part of my story.

Chapter Twenty-Six
CAMPAIGN TRAIL

Bob began attending city council meetings because he saw things occurring in our town that he thought could be improved. Without fail, he attended every monthly meeting. He had ideas, and he was frustrated. Some of his dissatisfaction must have spilled over to his fellow citizens and colleagues, because he began receiving encouragement to run for a position on the city council. I was one of his staunchest supporters. I thought this was a good idea, and I knew he would be an excellent candidate.

When he decided to throw his hat into the political arena, the first order of business was to get a petition and collect signatures of support for his candidacy. This was an easy task, because the citizens of Roseville welcomed a chance for change in city government. Many people happily supported his candidacy. I began making rounds to PTA meetings, asking for backing for my husband. I was active in the community and knew more people than Bob did. Most of his contacts were with business people in a nearby community where his business was located. I was a room mother at my children's school and actively involved with school activities; I had a heartfelt interest in education. The city of Roseville, primarily a blue-collar community with a population of sixty thousand in 1970, is where I had most of my contacts.

Having plowed ground for his candidacy among my school acquaintances, we then turned to the neighborhoods and shopping centers. I recruited my daughters and their friends. Here, I found a group of willing and enthusiastic campaigners. In the mall, Nicole, our youngest, did a little tap dance and sang a rhyme composed especially for the campaign, requesting votes for her daddy. Our three girls dressed up in red, white, and blue. Across the front of their shirts they wore ribbons with large bold letters that read "Vote for Bob Matuja." Since my husband was in the lumber business, there was no shortage of wooden sticks to make into placards announcing the candidacy of Bob Matuja for Roseville City Council. For the children, it was an education in the political process, as well as some social interaction and fun. These activities ended in a trip to McDonald's, a picnic in our backyard, and a swim in the pool. We also went door-to-door in the neighborhoods, passing out literature. For their efforts in this endeavor, the campaigners were paid a minimum wage. An adult volunteer, who provided both the supervision and transportation, drove them to each neighborhood. The atmosphere was happy and upbeat, with a sense of purpose and a desire to win uppermost in our minds.

Bob also went door-to-door in the community, introducing himself and presenting his agenda if elected. He won the election. We were pleased with the outcome, and our campaigners and supporters were jubilant. It was a happy ending for the citizens, both young and old, who worked hard during the campaign.

Bob began his term as a councilman, discussing his views and ideas on how the city should function. I found that I did not always agree with some of his decisions, and I started to express my opinions regarding city business. One day, he responded sarcastically, "Well, if you think you can do better, why don't you run?" To everyone's surprise, including my own, I accepted the challenge. I ran for a seat on the city council in hopes of launching my own political career. To this day, I don't know why I did it. Perhaps it was a challenge I couldn't refuse.

Chapter Twenty-Seven
STRANGE BEDFELLOWS

Having completed Bob's campaign two years earlier, I had a pretty good working knowledge of the political process. Once again, I took to the campaign trail. The difference this time was that I did not receive the same cooperation from my husband that he had received from me. Undaunted, I went forth and did my own campaigning and self-promotion.

I discovered that the idea of two people from the same family on the city council presented a detriment to my candidacy. I placed all of my effort into conveying the fact that I was an individual and that my hopes for the city and my way of thinking were my own. I anticipated that some citizens would try to argue that I would automatically think the same as my husband and follow his lead. In fact, one man asked me, "Why should we elect you? You'll just vote with your husband!" I fired back, "What's the difference if we happen to vote for the same thing? If the idea is good, I'm voting for the idea, not because my husband supported it." This man was a chauvinistic individual and difficult to convince. When asked if he would permit his wife to go door-to-door and campaign, he answered with a resounding, "Hell, no!" I explained to him that I wanted to make changes in the city. I told him that my husband was not wholly supportive of my candidacy but had suggested I should run for office. "That is why I am seeking your support," I said. Although I encountered this type of opposition, I did have a favorable amount of support from the people within the community who knew me

*My neighborhood campaign group. (Back row L–R) Jennifer,
Kim Kare, Leslie. (Front row, L–R) Patty Mihall, Nicole*

as a friend, a neighbor, a tireless campaigner, an independent thinker, and a school activist and volunteer.

One of the most difficult things for me was going door-to-door and tooting my own horn. When campaigning for my husband, I had no problem telling folks about my candidate and why I thought they should vote for him. Now, I was running for office, and I had to go about the business of telling the whole town just how wonderful I was and convince them to vote for me. My platform consisted of assuring them I would do what was necessary to improve city services while cutting unnecessary expenses. The philosophy by which I have lived my life is, Be true to your word. Do the right thing.

The enjoyable part of campaigning was meeting people in the community and observing the similarities and differences in their living conditions. One thing that everyone had in common was a sense of how important the family is and the necessity to preserve familial relationships.

As a result of my parents' lack of involvement in my formative years, I knew that it is important for children to know that family is there for them. If the children believe they have support, it empowers them to believe in themselves. I never regretted the time and energy I spent as an active participant in my children's lives. It all begins with family. Family support and a sense of belonging to this nucleus of caring people can enhance an individual's feeling of well-being. This allows children to feel comforted and safe. This spiral of connection affects one's life, which affects the community, and ultimately contributes to the success of this nation. All of these thoughts were with me as I campaigned for the opportunity to serve my community.

In addition to family ties, I realized through campaigning that there are other values that ground us as individual citizens. A basic building block of character is credibility. In and out of the family, being true to our word so people can trust us is an important personal quality that defines who we are. For me, the glue in working toward these values is my belief in God. I have relied on my Christian faith whenever confronted with a difficult decision. I have tried to practice what I believe both at home and in public life. I am proud that Bob and I have given our children a good foundation in the values of true citizenship.

Eventually, I won one of the open seats in the election for city council. I even came within three votes of first place. Chuck Thomas, a reporter for the Macomb Daily newspaper,

Husband-Wife Council Team Hardly Ever Pull Together

Detroit Free Press article after I won my city council seat

conducted research and found that Bob and I were the only husband and wife councilperson team in the state of Michigan, possibly in the country.

Although the campaign was not without its ups and downs, for the most part it was a rewarding experience. Our victory party was held in our backyard with all of the neighbor children who had tirelessly campaigned in attendance. We had a swimming party with lots of hot dogs and ice cream—it was a triumphant celebration. The adults who served as captains during the campaign also were present. Prizes were distributed to those who had handed out the most literature and covered the most ground. There were many stories to tell regarding happenings along the way. We were lauding a victory that was won with hard work and a commitment to making a difference—the American way!

*Michigan Week visit to Dearborn (L-R) Barbara
Haggerty, Mayor Leonard Haggerty, Mayor Orville
Hubbard (in wheelchair), Councilwoman Mary Matuja*

*Serving on the council. (L–R) Councilwoman Mary Matuja,
Mayor Leonard Haggerty, Councilman Bob Matuja*

Chapter Twenty-Eight
SERVING ON THE COUNCIL

With little time to bask in the win, I was off and running, buried in all that my new job entailed as an elected member of the Roseville City Council. Controversial issues came before the council at various points in my career. At the time of my election, the city was in a downward spiral and falling behind financially. We had to contain costs without increasing taxes, a challenging predicament for many communities.

There were issues with the police officers and firefighters merging and cross-training involved. Public safety was an important concern, and there were strong feelings and opinions on all sides. This new adventure was a learning process for me. I had to learn the procedure of the meetings and the necessity of adhering to the agenda. We were involved in budget planning and the adoption of many changes that would affect city services.

At home, I found my children were becoming more interested in the political process. The frustration of how slowly the government moves on many issues became an ongoing topic of our dinner conversations.

Some experiences on the city council were sad. It was heart-rending to attend the funerals of city employees or their family members. Working together, we became an extended family, caring deeply for the well-being of our associates. Other experiences on the city council were downright dangerous and frightening. We survived the threat of car bombs, twenty-four-hour police protection during gun threats, and several memorable and pesky residents who complained about everything under the sun. Yes, it was stressful, but it was also part of the job. I wanted to make a difference, and I tried my best to do so.

There were good times and happy moments as well. I sought to create a more unified attitude between city government and school administration. I believed it would contribute to a stronger foundation in the community if schools and the city would work together to educate the students. Since I was a staunch supporter of children and education, I was appointed chairperson for Student Government Day. My mission was to explain to the students how the city government worked. This was a joyful assignment, as I always looked forward to working with young people. Children have yet to disappoint me; I have a heightened sense of strength when I witness their commitment, enthusiasm, idealism, and energy. I always ended the event with the phrase, "The future is in good hands."

Another highlight of my tenure on the council was a mayor-exchange day with the city of Dearborn. As part of the day, we toured Greenfield Village and attended lunch at the Henry Ford Museum. We also toured Henry Ford's first home, which is a designated historical site. During the day, I met the mayor of Dearborn, Mayor Orville Hubbard. Mayor Hubbard recently had suffered a stroke and was in a wheelchair. Although he was unable to talk, he wanted to attend a brief ceremony to honor our exchange.

The mayor and I already had met, many years prior to that ceremony. The meeting occurred shortly after I had arrived in America. At that time my family lived in Dearborn, and I usually played with my friends on the playground located right next to Dearborn's City Hall. My new neighborhood friends took me to City Hall and showed everyone the picture of me and my mother on the front page with the headline: An American for Five Days; She Loves It. Slovak Girl Reunited with Mother Here after Ten Years.

Mayor Hubbard had already seen the article. He called for his secretary, who just happened to be Slovakian, and she filled in as an interpreter for us.

"So, young Mary, how do you like it in America?" Mayor Hubbard had asked.

"Oh, I like it very much!" I replied.

"What is it that you like?" he inquired.

"I like hot dogs, malted milk, and chocolate," I responded. He laughed and pulled some Hershey bars from his desk drawer to distribute to us. When we were old enough, we decided, we were definitely going to vote for him! We all thanked him for the chocolate and while we devoured the bars, he continued asking questions.

"What do you want to be when you grow up, Mary?"

I thought for a second and then I blurted out, "I want your job!"

He slapped his leg and bellowed out another hearty laugh. "You know, Mary, if you study and work hard, you can have my job." And another round of chocolate was shared.

We bid Mayor Hubbard and his secretary a quick good-bye and ran off to the playground. The mayor was a clever man; he won many votes that day.

As I reminded him about our first meeting when I was just a young girl, Mayor Hubbard listened intently. I noticed a tear run down his cheek as he recalled that day in his office many years ago. For so many years, he had been a loyal servant to his constituents. While I may not have agreed with all of his political positions, I shall never forget the two meetings with him and the kindness he expressed to me, both as a new citizen and as an elected official. I told him he had been an inspiration for me to run for public office and reminded him that I was back for his job. He smiled and nodded his head in affirmation.

My tenure in office with the Roseville City Council lasted eight years. It required me to be flexible by listening to all the different sides of an issue, while at the same time being steadfast when the right solution presented itself. My principles and personal beliefs came under much scrutiny and were tested often. Politics is not a career for the faint of heart.

In my humble opinion, it is virtually impossible to be a lifelong politician and not make compromises along the way. And this ability to compromise can be perceived as a weakening of one's integrity. That is why I am vehemently in favor of term limitations, with eight years being the maximum anyone is allowed to serve. This restriction would eliminate self-service and help maintain public service. Holding public office shouldn't become a career but rather an opportunity to serve and contribute the best one has to offer. Running for office is open to everyone from every walk of life—what a great country!

Although the city council handled myriad issues during my tenure, one experience stands out in my memory.

On a bright, hot summer day in August, I received a call from a citizen who informed me that the garbage in her neighborhood hadn't been picked up, and she didn't want to smell it all weekend. I promised her I would make sure it was picked up. I tried unsuccessfully to reach someone at the Department of Public Works (DPW). The DPW employees were on a slow-down because their negotiations were not progressing to their liking, and the union was threatening to strike. I drove to the Department of Public Works building, wanting to know why the garbage wasn't getting picked up. I told them I had promised a citizen that the refuse in her neighborhood would be collected. They shrugged their shoulders, stating that they didn't have enough manpower.

I didn't want to go back on my word after I had assured the citizen her garbage would be picked up. I went home and gingerly approached my husband, telling him about the problem. He was working on the girls' playhouse roof when I interrupted him. I told him about the situation, and he said, "Well, what do you want me to do?" I told him that I promised the lady that her garbage would be picked up. "I can't go back on my word. Do you think maybe we could get the lumberyard pickup truck and just pick up the garbage in the neighborhood ourselves? It's only a few houses," I said. I could tell he wasn't too happy with me but he was a supportive husband and a good sport about it.

We picked up the truck and headed for the neighborhood with the garbage heap. Since the temperature was in the nineties, the entire subdivision reeked of smelly garbage. Bob said, "I thought you said a few houses."

And I snapped back, "I thought there were only a few houses!"

"Okay," he said, "you wanted equal rights, so I'll drive, you pitch!"

And on that hot Saturday afternoon in August you could find us collecting garbage in that neighborhood. When the back of the truck was filled, I jumped into the truck and headed for the DPW yard. To our surprise, the employees had locked the gates, preventing us from placing the garbage in the Dumpster. We decided to dump the garbage in front of the gates and then left to pick up more. By the time we were done, there was a mountain of garbage in front of those gates. The citizens were elated; the DPW employees were not. They had to remove the garbage on Monday morning in order to get through the gates.

I promised Bob that I would not do something like that to him again. We couldn't get back home fast enough, and the subsequent shower seemed like heaven on earth. We still laugh about it. I am now more appreciative of the work the DPW employees do. It's like that old adage: "Do not criticize unless you have walked a mile in someone else's shoes."

I also had an opportunity to ride in a police car for a day and experience what police officers go through. The only department I didn't work with was the fire department. During one contentious issue about merging the public safety units, a firefighter said to me, "I hope you have a long hose at your house." I thought perhaps I should stay off the fire trucks.

When Bob's term of office was up, he chose not to run again. His decision pleased me. I had two years left to serve, and they proved to be truly difficult years, full of stressful situations and upheaval. I was glad when I could finally say good-bye to those days of politics.

However, during my tenure on the council, I also served on many boards and commissions. Among them were the Macomb County Planning Commission and Michigan Works. I was honored to serve as chair for three consecutive years for Michigan Works, and I made many

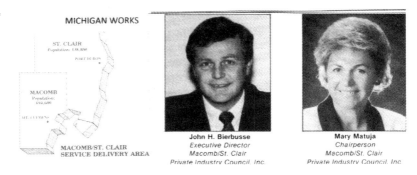

Brochure literature with photo of Executive Director John Bierbusse and me.

lasting friendships there. I also served as chairperson for the Roseville Schools Enrichment Program.

In addition, I served on the board for the Michigan Cancer Foundation, now known as the Karmanos Cancer Institute, and I continue serving on this board today. The irony is that in 2008, I was diagnosed with endometrial cancer. I was treated at the Karmanos Cancer Institute, and I am grateful to Dr. Deppe and his fine staff for the care and compassion they showered upon me during my surgery and recovery. I am committed to work to help eradicate this disease. I continue to raise funds and support those who are on the front lines, both in research and direct care given to cancer patients. My respect and heartfelt wishes go out to them for their work to bring about an end to the intolerable pain and heartache caused by cancer. Help cancer fail—this phrase was coined by the late chairman of the Michigan Cancer Foundation, David Hermalin. Sadly, he himself succumbed to this dreadful disease.

Chapter Twenty-Nine
MOVING ON

We were at that point in our lives where we felt ready to move to a new community. Bob and I had decided we would serve two terms at eight years each. He served as mayor pro tem for two years, and I followed by serving for the next two years. When my term ended, I wanted to focus my energies on creating a new home for us. The citizens of Roseville continued to pressure me to run again, promising support, but moving out of Roseville seemed like the right thing to do. It would also enable us to catch our breath.

Becoming private citizens again was necessary for our own sake and for the welfare of our family. We purchased a lot in Grosse Pointe Shores, Michigan. This seemed like a logical move, as our lot was two blocks from Bob's parents' home; we wanted to be close to his aging parents. The village of Grosse Pointe Shores is a small, quaint community located on lovely Lake St. Clair, with a population of about three thousand residents. Ontario, Canada can be seen across the lake. To our delight, we found that our new community had adopted the public safety concept of public protection. This was one form of service we tried in vain to implement when we were both council members in Roseville. We had been persecuted by the firefighters' union for attempting to implement the idea of combining police and fire services into one department. On the other hand, Grosse Pointe Shores was actually the first community to embrace this concept and had been functioning well for over one hundred years.

We broke ground for our new home after months of applying for a variance. We talked to and petitioned our soon-to-be neighbors for their signatures to permit us a five foot variance on the side set-back. We needed the variance because Lake Shore Road curves, which configured our lot into a pie shape instead of a rectangle. I collected the signatures and at the same time had an opportunity to meet our new neighbors. The variance was granted, and I was one happy camper to know that one day soon, we would be able to move into our new home, away from the political arena.

I immersed myself totally in choosing paint colors, wallpaper, appliances, flooring, and drapes. It was a ton of work. It was exciting and a delight, except getting Bob to agree with some of my choices was decidedly a chore. One evening I got so angry that I dumped the wallpaper books, all samples, and drapery remnants on the floor and resigned my position as interior decorator. In an instant, the job was reinstated to me totally, and all decisions were mine alone. Well . . . almost. The lion had retreated; he only wanted to roar.

The home was finally completed, except for the landscaping. I enjoyed working with the landscape architect to choose the trees: lindens along the side street that were shaped into cones, flowering pear trees along the boulevard on Lake Shore, pink dogwood and azaleas along the front, with a hedge of yews, birch trees, and white pine. We had gardens with an array of colors, ranging from purple to lavender to salmon to pinks. Perennials were mixed with annuals. Bob had looked at the architect's design and howled, "You can't even see the house; this place will be a dense forest that you won't be able to find your way out of!"

So it was back to the drawing board. We began cutting down the forest, coming to an amicable agreement of sorts. Half of the trees had to go, but I could still appreciate the beauty of the forest and gardens, rewarding us with endless blossoms and the sweet smells of success.

After settling into our new home, I was beginning to get restless; I needed an outlet. I accepted an appointment to the Grosse Pointe Shores Improvement Foundation to help improve and enhance the community around us. I noticed that the street signs and lighting were looking a bit rusty, and I dedicated my efforts to updating the lighting along the boulevard on Lake Shore Road and planting seascape gardens along the waterfront. The ornamental lighting has since been duplicated in neighboring communities. The lighting and gardens were donated by residents, along with a sprinkler system. Board members John Boll, Ron Lamparter, and I traveled door-to-door, soliciting funds to install a sprinkler system for Lake Shore Road foliage. The results were beautiful and gratifying. Even Hollywood agrees, as Clint Eastwood's movie *Gran Torino* included a shot of the car driving down the picturesque boulevard while the credits were rolling. I say, "Hooray for Clint Eastwood and hooray for community activists!"

The Grosse Pointe Shores Improvement Foundation was instrumental in creating many improvements. The village administration and the council cooperated, working hand in hand for a common cause. The result: a beautiful hamlet by the sea.

Soon after that I gladly accepted the next opportunity presented to me. Mayor Edmund M. Brady, Jr. asked me if I would work on the Village of Grosse Pointe Shores Planning Commission. The city council approved my appointment, and I have continued to serve on this commission for thirty years.

Good things happen when citizens work together. Sadly, I have seen self-serving individuals attempt to destroy the beauty and good works created by hardworking citizens within a community. But most often, I have seen good people work together for good causes. I am grateful for the opportunities I have had to fulfill my dedication to a country that I love and a community that I am proud to represent and be a part of.

After a short hiatus from politics, I reluctantly accepted an appointment to the Grosse Pointe Township Board of Commissioners. I served as clerk for a year. The supervisor retired and a vacancy occurred; I was the first woman appointed to fill the position as supervisor of Grosse Pointe Township. There I was, in the political arena once again. Elections were held every two years. I served for six years, and I was

Grosse Pointe Township trustees (L–R) Robert Graziani; Dr. James Cooper;
Mary Matuja, supervisor; Gary Mitchell; Donald Haigh

the only woman to serve in this position (and the last). While supervisor, I voted in favor of incorporation and consequently voted myself out of a job. I later quipped at the council meeting that I was possibly the first supervisor who "pink-slipped" herself. With incorporation, we became the village of Grosse Pointe Shores, a "Michigan City" designation. In 2010, I retired my gavel. I was fortunate to have met and worked with so many interesting and outstanding citizens. I am proud to have contributed and hope I made a difference.

Planning Commission, Village of Grosse Pointe Shores (L-R) Gary Mitchell,
Gary Gula, Patrick McCarroll, Chairwoman Mary Matuja, Allen Broad,
Michael Monahan, Council Representative Robert Gesell

Chapter Thirty
FINALE

Dear Grandfather,

There was a time when words came pouring out of me as I was telling my story. I could hardly write them down fast enough. But now, as it is time to bring it all to a close, I am struggling for the right words to express my feelings, especially for you and for Grandmother.

How can I thank two extraordinary people who were instrumental in molding me into the person I am today? You fed, protected, and directed my life through a most crucial period, during one of the most perilous times in world history. You poured your heart and soul into raising, encouraging, teaching, and loving me. And all the while, there was little or no food to eat and no place to live. I can only imagine the worry that constantly tormented you. How would we survive through the war? How could you keep me from harm? How could you let me go, knowing you might never see me again? And then there were the letters I wrote to you from America. How did you bear my letters, begging to come back, telling you how much I hated my new home, and asking why you abandoned me? Only today can I fully understand the pain that was camouflaged in your responses, always encouraging me. Be patient, Marya. Study hard, Marya. Education is the one thing that no one can take from you, Marya.

I wonder what you would say to me today. Would you remind me that you worried about what would have become of me if I hadn't left for America? Would you tell me you cried when reading my letters about how much I missed you?

I hope that the capricious little girl didn't disappoint the dream you dreamed for her. My dearest Grandfather, I am sorry that I could not write this letter when you could read it. It has taken many years for me to realize what an important part of my life you were. As a grandmother myself now, I can understand the depth of the sacrifices and hardship you experienced for me.

After all these years, I have never forgotten my promise to return to you. This book is the fulfillment of that promise. In its words, I have not only returned to our years together, but I have brought fellow travelers as well.

As I write this last chapter of my life story, the tears are soaking the paper and making the words illegible. My feelings of gratitude have overwhelmed me. How proud I was to walk hand in hand with you to church every Sunday. You have been the shining light permeating my life. The lessons you taught me will help mold future generations of your kin. They will live on through my daughters and grandchildren. The events in my life changed me, but those incredible experiences also changed the perspective of my family. My children and grandchildren possess the motivation to make differences in their communities and in the world. They will embrace people from other lands, get involved in schools, attempt public service, and teach and instill the values that you taught me. I will always be thankful and proud that you raised me.

Whatever combination of events created my personal path through Czechoslovakia, Poland, and on to America, I am grateful. The person I am today—the woman who has been able to remember the details of Gypsy dances, exploding bombs, shoes lost in the mud—that person, me, your little Marya, is still so very proud to say . . . Hello America!

Always,
Your loving little Marya

Grandma and Grandpa Šafran's resting place

Mary Matuja

MARY (HOĆ-BOBAK) MATUJA immigrated to the United States in 1949 at the age of ten. She was unable to speak English and made the long journey alone to be reunited with her mother, from whom she was separated during World War II when she was four months old. Mary became an advocate for educational excellence and believed that foreign language should be taught in elementary grades. She introduced an enrichment program by enlisting citizens in the community to share their knowledge and expertise with young students and for which she received the Roseville Schools award for Excellence in Education. She is listed in the *Who's Who of American Women* as well as the *World's Who's Who of Women*. She attended college, became a Patricia Stevens model in Detroit, Michigan, and in Canada, and performed with an international dance troupe. She won the Miss Michigan Water Sports title, which qualified her to compete in the Miss Michigan—Miss America pageant. She was elected councilwoman and mayor pro tem in Roseville, Michigan. She was elected supervisor to one of the premier communities in the United States, Grosse Pointe Township, Michigan.

She continues her involvement in the community as a visiting lecturer on WWII and immigration.

Mary remembers that as a young girl in Czechoslovakia, she was often told stories of America and its streets "paved in gold." Unfortunately, she didn't find this to be true, but what she did find were golden opportunities for those who choose to seize them. For her, being a true American goes deeper than merely holding citizenship. She believes it has a special meaning that requires, at the very least, a sincere appreciation for the vast freedoms and opportunities this country offers. She is proud of her heritage and very proud and grateful to be an American.